500 RECIPES FOR HOME-MADE WINES AND DRINKS

by Marguerite Patten

HAMLYN
LONDON·NEW YORK·SYDNEY·TORONTO

Contents

Cover photograph by Paul Williams

Published by The Hamlyn Publishing Group Limited
London · New York · Sydney · Toronto
Astronaut House, Feltham, Middlesex, England

Revised edition 1971
Fourteenth impression 1980

ISBN 0 600 34353 7

Printed and bound in Great Britain by
Morrison & Gibb Ltd., London and Edinburgh

Introduction

This book is perhaps a little out of the ordinary in that many of the recipes revive those wines and beverages that used to be made habitually in the kitchens of Britain. Home-made wine making is something that has to be done with care. You need to bring a slightly scientific approach to this as the right blending of ingredients, speed of fermentation, etc., all help to produce a first class wine.

If you feel that wine making is not for you, there are still many things which I hope will interest you in this book. Included are drinks, both alcoholic and non-alcoholic for special occasions, delicious home-made liqueurs and traditional mulled drinks, enabling you to produce something a little out of the ordinary when you entertain.

Quantities to serve

In many of the recipes in this book, you will find the quantities given. Naturally these are approximate as the size of glasses vary. Sometimes the quantities may appear a little misleading as in a punch, which does not contain a vast quantity of liquid yet seems to serve a surprising number of people. This is because the contents of a punch are either strongly flavoured or rather potent and one therefore assumes that less will be offered.

In the case of milk shakes, the portions are based on a ½-pint tumbler or goblet but even these vary a little if it is a particularly rich milk shake, when a slightly smaller glass can be used.

Some Useful Facts and Figures

Notes on metrication

In case you wish to convert quantities into metric measures, the following tables give a comparison.

Solid measures

Ounces	Approx. grams to nearest whole figure	Recommended conversion to nearest unit of 25
1	28	25
2	57	50
3	85	75
4	113	100
5	142	150
6	170	175
7	198	200
8	227	225
9	255	250
10	283	275
11	312	300
12	340	350
13	368	375
14	396	400
15	425	425
16 (1 lb)	454	450
17	482	475
18	510	500
19	539	550
20 (1¼ lb)	567	575

Note: When converting quantities over 20 oz first add the appropriate figures in the centre column, then adjust to the nearest unit of 25. As a general guide, 1 kg (1000 g) equals 2·2 lb or about 2 lb 3 oz. This method of conversion gives good results in nearly all cases, although in certain pastry and cake recipes a more accurate conversion is necessary to produce a balanced recipe.

Liquid measures

Imperial	Approx. millilitres to nearest whole figure	Recommended millilitres
¼ pint	142	150
½ pint	283	300
¾ pint	425	450
1 pint	567	600
1½ pints	851	900
1¾ pints	992	1000 (1 litre)

Oven temperatures

The table below gives recommended equivalents.

	°C	°F	Gas Mark
Very cool	110	225	¼
	120	250	½
Cool	140	275	1
	150	300	2
Moderate	160	325	3
	180	350	4
Moderately hot	190	375	5
	200	400	6
Hot	220	425	7
	230	450	8
Very hot	240	475	9

Notes for American and Australian users

In America the 8-oz measuring cup is used. In Australia metric measures are now used in conjunction with the standard 250-ml measuring cup. The Imperial pint, used in Britain and Australia, is 20 fl oz, while the American pint is 16 fl oz. It is important to remember that the Australian tablespoon differs from both the British and American tablespoons. The British standard tablespoon, which has been used throughout this book, holds 17·7 ml, the American 14·2 ml, and the Australian 20 ml. A teaspoon holds approximately 5 ml in all three countries.

To Choose, Serve and Store Wine

To choose wine

Although in the past there have been certain rules on serving the correct wines with certain foods, people today are far more adaptable and the tendency is to serve the wines which are most enjoyed by both the host and his guests.

Cocktail party

Nowadays, when help is not so readily available, it is quite a good idea to limit the selection of drinks and to have a few glasses of sherry, vermouth and gin already filled before your guests arrive. Have bottles of tonic water and a syphon of soda available.

Sherry

Give people a choice of dry and sweet. The driest is Tio Pepe, but as many people find this too dry, Amontillado or a Rosa are good choices. Walnut brown sherry is an ideal sweet sherry.

Vermouth

Have a choice of sweet and dry.

Dubonnet

Serve with ice and lemon, or as a long drink serve with soda or bitter lemon.

Cinzano

Red or white.

Campari

A drink that like Cinzano is becoming increasingly popular.

You can, of course, mix your own cocktails and suggestions are given on pages 65–69.

Buffet party

This is very similar to a cocktail party, except that food as well as drink is available. This means it is doubly advisable to have some glasses of drinks already filled before your guests arrive, so that they can immediately choose what they would like.

The selection of drinks could also be very similar to a cocktail party, except on a special occasion such as a wedding buffet or a twenty-first birthday party, when champagne and a bigger selection of wines can be given.

You could, of course, have a centre piece of one of the punches or cups on pages 69–82.

Dinner party

Your choice of wines will, of course, depend on the amount of money you wish to spend.

It is usual for the guests to have an aperitif before dinner and you may care to offer a selection of sherries, or leave them to choose from a wider range of drinks.

More information about wine is given below, but here are a few general hints.

A red wine is best served at room temperature, so keep this in the room for some little time before dinner.

White wine is best when it is cool, but not iced. If you have offered sherry as an aperitif, it can be served at the beginning of the meal with the hors d'oeuvre or soup. Most people prefer a pale or medium sherry, such as Amontillado and Rosa, or Tio Pepe which is very dry. Although medium sweet sherry is not particularly good to accompany soup, an Oloroso or Idolo can be chosen.

With the Fish Course

Choose a White Burgundy (Chablis) a Hock (Liebfraumilch), a Moselle or a dry Graves.

With Chicken or Turkey

Choose either the same wines as above or have Claret (a red Bordeaux—i.e. Pomerol or St. Emilion). Choose one of the Château range for a special occasion, such as Château Margaux. Or a Médoc or a red Burgundy—Pommard is very good.

With Duck, Goose or Roast Meat

As a rule, people have a Claret or red Burgundy, but if preferred have a white wine.

With the Sweet

A sweet Sauternes is very good. A sparkling Burgundy is also excellent.

With coffee

Choose a 'full-blooded' wine. Have a port wine, Marsala, Madeira or a sweet sherry.

Liqueurs to serve with or after coffee

There is a very large selection to choose from. The most usual is brandy (served in a warm glass), Crème de Menthe, Drambuie (whisky liqueur), or a fruit flavoured brandy such as apricot, peach or cherry.

Tia Maria, a coffee flavoured liqueur, has also become extremely popular.

Decanting wines

Red wine is placed in a decanter because:—

1 The wine is separated from the sediment which has formed at the base of the bottle.
2 The wine comes into greater contact with the air which gives it a better flavour.

Red wine can be served in a wine cradle which means slow steady pouring and ensures the sediment is not disturbed.

To decant, very slowly pour the wine from the bottle into the container. Do this very steadily and slowly while the bottle is held in a horizontal position.

If the bottle of wine is stood upright for several hours before decanting, the sediment will fall to the bottom.

If you put a light behind the bottle as you pour, you will see quite clearly when the wine begins to get cloudy.

The 'wasted' wine at the bottom of the bottle can perfectly well be used in cooking.

Cleaning decanters

Decanters which are used very regularly are apt to become discoloured. Here are various methods of cleaning them.

1 Put a little detergent and water into the decanter and allow to soak. Shake from time to time. You will probably find this cleans it quite well.
2 White vinegar and salt put into the bottom of the decanter, topped with water and left to stand is often successful if the stain is obstinate.
3 Break up egg shells into fairly small pieces and put in the bottom of the decanter covered with lemon juice. Leave for two days, shaking from time to time. You will find the eggshells dissolve in the lemon juice and at the end of this time the glass should be sparkling and bright.

Storing wines

Although this book is primarily concerned with making your own drinks, many of these depend not only on the wines you make, but the ones you buy, and in order to keep them in the best condition, they must be stored at the right temperature.

If your house has no cellar in which the wine can be stored, a cupboard under the stairs, or something similar, can be used, but care should be taken that in both summer and winter the temperature does not exceed 55°F. It is possible to buy quite inexpensive wine racks in which the bottles can be placed. This means that they can be stored on their sides—in this way the wines are in the best condition for keeping.

Red wines need longer to mature than white wines, so it is better to choose more of these if planning to keep a store. Port wine is also a very good wine to have in stock.

To Choose and Decorate Glasses

To choose glasses

Cocktails and martinis are generally served in a shallow glass.

Champagne is served in proper champagne glasses.

Sherry is served in a small glass.

Red wine is served in a glass with a fairly short stem.

White wine can be served in either a long stemmed glass or the same shape as red wine.

Port wine is served in a small bowl shaped glass.

Brandy is served in large tulip shaped glasses.

Liqueurs are served in specially made liqueur glasses which are very tiny.

Beer can be served either in a tankard or a tumbler.

Lager is generally served in a special lager glass, rather taller and narrower than a tumbler.

To look after your glasses

Be careful when placing glasses with fragile stems into a dish-washer, as they may tip and the stems break.

If your glassware is very valuable, wash up in a plastic washing up bowl, and protect the glasses from any knocks they may receive by laying a cloth at the bottom of the bowl.

Wash glasses up in a warm but not hot, soapy or detergent lather. Rinse very well in clear water and then either leave to dry or polish carefully with a clean 'non-fluffy' tea towel. For extra sparkle, give a final rub with soft tissue paper.

Before putting glasses on to the table, give them a gentle rub with a soft cloth.

To frost edges of glasses

Some drinks, such as fruit cups and cold punches, look even more attractive if served in a frosted glass. There are several ways of doing this.

1 Damp the rims of the glasses with cold water and roll in castor sugar.
2 For a thicker frosting, brush the rims with slightly beaten egg white, and dip in sugar.
3 For a white frosting, use egg whites and sieved icing sugar.
4 For a coloured frosting, work a few drops of vegetable colouring into castor or granulated sugar and let this dry before use.

Decoration of glasses

Mention is made above of frosting the rims of glasses, but your glasses or tumblers can look much more interesting if you have a colourful decoration with your drink.

Choose slices of lemon or orange. Slit these a little so they balance safely on the rim of the glass.

Pare long narrow strips of orange or lemon peel and put these on top of the drink just before serving.

If the juice from the lemon or orange peel is squeezed into the drink it adds a strong flavour to the rest of the drink.

Making Your Own Wine

It is not legal to sell home-made wine. It is for home consumption only and you should not therefore offer it for sale under any circumstances. This includes any sale for your Women's organisations, Church, etc.

Alcohol content of home-made wine

The alcoholic content of home-made wines, ciders, meads, etc. is often very high so please do not offer them to young people in the mistaken idea it is a home-made drink and does not compare with the wines you buy. In many cases a matured home-made wine is more potent.

What wine making entails

Making wine is not really a very difficult process.

It is, however, a process where proportions of sugar, etc., should be followed carefully.

These are the stages you need to follow:

1 Extract the juice from the fruit or vegetable, flowers or cereal.
  In most cases this is done by putting any of these into the container and pouring over boiling water. In a few cases you need to heat the mixture, but this is specified in the particular recipe.

2 You then need to press (see page 10 for further details). The object of doing this is to extract the maximum amount of juice.

3 Leave the mixture to infuse for several days and you can continue pressing during this period for the more juice you can get from the fruit, etc., the better the flavour will be.

4 Having left the mixture to infuse pour off the liquid and add sugar, yeast and any flavourings recommended in the recipe.

5 Then put it into the container to ferment (see page 11). After a period of time, with the help of the yeast, the mixture starts to bubble or ferment. The period of time will vary, but on an average takes several weeks. In a few cases it will happen very quickly—an indication of this is given in the individual recipe.

6 Should you wish to have a sparkling wine (see page 12), bottle the mixture before fermentation has ceased. If a still wine is desired, wait until fermentation has completely finished before bottling.
  Directions for bottling are on page 12.

7 Strain the juice very carefully before bottling (see details about straining on page 10) and then the wine will be ready to store.

Equipment for wine making

Do not be frightened into thinking you must have very elaborate equipment for making wine. Obviously if you intend to make a great deal of wine for home consumption, you will invest in the rather special equipment, but for making just one or two batches, it is surprising how you can improvise with the articles you have in your own home. Below you will find the things that will be required.

Wooden board

For the preparation of fruit. Make sure it contains no splinters, etc.

Stainless steel and silver utensils

For chopping fruit, vegetables, etc., and for containers.

Containers

The containers for fruit, vegetables, etc., and water can be any of the following:

Glass

Remember you are using hot water, so it must be very strong.

Polythene

Most polythene cannot stand boiling water, but it must be remembered that by the time the water goes over the fruit it will no longer be boiling.

Sound enamelware

You must have no chips whatsoever in enamelware.

Utensils and receptacles should not have been used for other purposes than cooking and they must be very carefully cleaned before being used. If using soap or soapless detergents, rinse out very thoroughly. If you have to heat in a pan as is the case with a few ingredients, you may find that you have to do it in several batches to give space.

Extracting the juice

You can use wooden spoons for soft fruit, or an ordinary vegetable masher if wished, but it is possible to buy fruit presses in the shops now.

Straining

For straining the juice in the first place, a large colander is ideal. Your ordinary one is adequate. When the juice has been strained, it should be put back again into the original container for the addition of yeast.

When the juice, etc., has been blended with the sugar, it is then strained into the container to ferment and as a colander is not fine enough at this stage use a straining bag, a filter bag in felt or ordinary linen filter bags; all of which are easily obtainable from department stores. You may, however, like to strain through several thicknesses of flannel, which is quite satisfactory. The modern fine terylene or nylon materials are also suitable as is butter muslin if several thicknesses are used.

Fermentation

For the process of fermentation you can use either a wooden cask or a glass storage jar complete with its cork which remains a fairly cheap item to buy. You may be able to advertise for a wooden cask and buy this second-hand, but it can be purchased by ordering from proper wine stockists. Instead of a glass or wooden container, you could use polythene which is just as efficient. Many people, however, prefer stoneware or earthenware with a bung, i.e. type of stopper, which is ideal. You can also buy jars with taps which enable you to draw off the wine very easily.

During fermentation, as will be explained on page 11, the container must be filled to the brim, so never buy a container too large for the amount of wine you intend to make and remember you have to have a little wine left over for filling up, so if you make wine to fill a gallon container, you should really have over a gallon of wine.

Never buy containers that cannot be cleaned (see directions below) and never use containers like a cask where vinegar has been stored.

During the process of fermentation, for really first-class results, a fermentation lock does enable you to control the escape of the carbon dioxide bubbles. These locks are obtainable at reasonable prices. They can be obtained to fit into the cork of a jar. With a cask, of course, your fermentation is controlled by the tap. A tap is also sometimes included on a jar. Some people have successfully controlled the flow of bubbles by covering jars with very thick paper with a small slit in it.

After, or just before fermentation has ceased if a sparkling wine is desired, the wine has to be strained into bottles. In a few cases it is better to syphon the wine off rather than strain it. However, most wines go through a strainer and you can use your linen bags, etc., as mentioned previously. If not completely clear, follow directions for using isinglass on page 10, or put through filter papers. These are reasonably cheap.

Tray

A tray or other utensil is required to stand under the bottle, cask, etc., to catch froth as it overflows.

Bottles

When you know you are going to make wine you can probably save bottles from the wine merchant. They must be very strong if you intend to put a sparkling wine into them (see page 12). Make sure they are absolutely clean. You can buy special bottle cleaning brushes for this purpose. Use new corks. If you are making a lot of wine, it is worth investing in a hand corking machine, which is a relatively inexpensive item.

To get the wine into the bottles you will need a wide-necked glass, enamel or polythene funnel.

Labels

You will want to label your wine neatly and attractive labels can be obtained from stationers or from the firms who sell wine making equipment.

Wires

As explained under sparkling wine (see page 12), owing to the fact that fermentation has not ceased you will need to wire the corks in position and you can either use the proper looped wire or thin galvanised wire.

Cleaning containers

It has been stressed that your containers for storing fruit, and wines, etc., must be clean, but if you are using jars or casks that have been stored for a long time, you must do more than just wash them out with water.

One of the best ways of cleaning jars or bottles is to fill them with plenty of clean water and put in approximately 4–6 Campden tablets, plus 1 tablespoon of citric acid. Both of these are obtainable from a chemist. Cover and leave for as long as possible. Use a firm clean brush and brush round, emptying out the solution after several days. If the jar still appears not to be as clean as you would wish, repeat the process. A cask is a little more difficult to clean. A little ordinary soda and boiling water mixed together can be poured into the cask. Use no more than 3 oz. soda to 1 gallon water. Leave for 1–2 days, then strain out and rinse in several lots of clean cold water. To make sure the cask is in a good condition for making wine, pour a little cheap wine or cider into it and turn it round so your wood becomes impregnated with the liquid. In this way you make sure the wine will not have any flavour from the wood of the cask.

If the wine has been made before in the cask this is not necessary. It is a wise precaution to sterilise jars and casks if the juices have to stand in them for a long time. This can be done by warming a jar, then filling it with boiling water. Allow to cool and repeat a second time. You can do exactly the same with a cask.

To sterilise corks, which can be the source of mould or infection, wash in plenty of clean hot, not boiling, water. If the cork seems very tight and a bad fit you can soften it by steeping in cold water for some hours.

Pressing out the juice for wine

The work you put into pressing the juice is very important for, unless you extract this thoroughly, your wine will not be full-bodied. If you are using a wooden spoon, it does mean pressing hard at the side of the container unless the fruit or vegetables are very soft.

If you are using a vegetable presser, do this very firmly. With a proper fruit presser, it is, of course, a simple matter.

Straining your fruit or vegetable juices

A great deal of needless worry can be caused by inadequate straining of the fruit or vegetable juices. If you do not carry this out properly your wine will not have the proper clarity needed. You will find on page 10 suggestions for the way to strain the juice, but the way you arrange the muslin or support the bag is important. If you are not using the proper support with a jelly bag, you should attach the bag to the legs of an up-turned stool so the juice can trickle through. The correct support is not very expensive to buy and is extremely useful. Never try to squeeze the bag or push through the juice as though you were making a purée. If you do the infusion will immediately become clouded. After a time, paper, muslin, etc., ceases to be efficient and should be renewed.

Using sugar in wine making

Unless stated to the contrary, white granulated sugar should be used. In some recipes, however, brown sugar is recommended and demerara is the best choice.

Using golden syrup in making wines

It is possible to use golden syrup instead of sugar in wine making.

It is perhaps not quite so good in wine making because it does tend to alter the colour very slightly, but it does give a rather rich flavour. The warmed golden syrup is added to the recipes in place of sugar and exactly the same amount should be used.

To clear wine

If, after straining, your wine does not look clear, check carefully that you are using a fine enough filter. It may well be that an extra two thicknesses of muslin, etc. will immediately make a difference.

If, after fermentation and straining it is not clear, then you must use isinglass or egg white to ensure the wine is perfect to look at. The white of one egg is sufficient for several gallons. Whisk it until firm, add to the wine in the container and leave for 24 hours. You should then be satisfied with the result. If isinglass is used dissolve in a very small quantity of cold water, using $\frac{1}{4}$ oz. isinglass to each gallon of wine. Add to the wine and leave for several weeks, after which time you should have a perfect result.

It may well be that the haze or cloudiness in the wine is caused by the sediment which is disturbed by tipping the container when straining the wine. This is why many people prefer to syphon rather than strain a wine.

There are actual faults in the wine that can cause a haze and this is a little difficult to rectify. In a dry wine it may be because it is becoming a little vinegary, a condition which will get worse rather than better, so the wine must be used at once.

In a sweet wine, it could be because the yeast is providing a special growth. In this case the best solution is to syphon the wine carefully into a new container, leaving the growth behind. When storing in bottles as detailed on page 12, wine racks are the best to use as they allow the sediment to drop to the heel, i.e. the base, of the bottle.

Preparing the mixture for fermentation

1 Fill the cask or jars to the brim—but always keep back a little of the juice to fill up the cask or jar as the fermenting liquid spills over.
2 Put a tray under the cask or jar or stand it in a larger container so you catch the overflow. The overflow cannot be used in the wine.
3 Casks or jars should be lightly covered during the process of fermentation, so the liquid froth or scum, as it is often called, can overflow, and at the same time as much air as possible is excluded.
4 The proper container seals are described on page 9 but if you are using large wide topped jars you could use thick firm paper, tied down, with a slit in the top.

Storage conditions for jars, casks, etc., of wine

The correct temperature for storing wines during fermentation, etc., is given below, but it must be stressed that not only temperature but humidity, etc., is nearly as important as the temperature. The room should be dry and clean. If you are storing in a rarely used room, it should be well cleaned before the wine is put in so there is no fear of dampness or mould forming.

The process of fermentation

Fermentation of the ingredients in wine making is the growth of minute organisms in the mixture, which causes the change in the juices of the fruits, etc., and in time produces a pleasant tasting liquid which we recognise as wine.

This is a long process, varying with the different fruits or vegetables from 2–4 months.

One important point to remember is that when yeast is put into the ingredients for wine you are adding a live organism, and like any plant it needs the right conditions in order to 'grow'. Ideally the temperature at which you store the bulk wine for fermentation should be between 65°F. and 80°F. See page 8 for containers to use. Some people find as low as 60°F. quite successful, but you should be careful not to exceed 80°F., and it is quite wrong to put the containers into direct sunlight. When storing bottles of wine the temperature should then be only about 55°F. or 60°F.

In the average home it may be difficult to find the right place to store the casks or containers of wine during fermentation though the bottom of a warm airing cupboard is quite a good place —do however test the temperature of any storage place, for yeast, like any other growing plant, could be killed by excess cold or heat.

During fermentation you should regularly see how the wine is progressing. As you will see from individual recipes the process varies in time a great deal, but well matured fruit, etc. will give juices that ferment reasonably quickly; poor quality fruits etc., take longer. *If you find the juices fermenting slowly, i.e. bubbling very slowly indeed* it may well be that the temperature is a little too low, and you will have a better result if the container is moved to a slightly warmer position. If you still find that in spite of the correct storage conditions the wine is not fermenting successfully, then it might well be advisable to add a little yeast—use half the amount originally recommended in the recipe— and after a day or so you should then find successful results. *If on the other hand you find the juices fermenting quickly, i.e. bubbling, very quickly indeed and looking like a froth*, it is fairly certain that the storage conditions are too hot, and you should find a cooler place.

The right fermentation is to produce even and continuous bubbles.

To produce a dry wine

Use the minimum amount of sugar in the

recipe generally about 2–2½ lb. per gallon of juice.

The addition of lemon juice also helps to give sharpness to the wine. Remember that if you reduce the amount of sugar too much you produce an over-tart, unpleasant flavour to the wine.

To produce a sweet wine

Use the maximum amount of sugar in the recipe—this is generally about 3–3½ lb. per gallon of juice.

Remember that if you increase the amount of sugar *too* much you produce an unpleasantly sickly drink.

To give sparkling wines

Most of the wine recipes give a still wine, but if you wish a sparkling wine follow the directions for making, adjust the sugar for a dry sparkling or sweet sparkling wine, then allow fermentation to continue as in the recipe, but do not wait for it to finish completely.

Strain the wines into bottles. Because the wines will produce gas as they ferment in the bottles the corks must be wired on. If you are obtaining other utensils, etc., from a store selling wine making equipment you can obtain suitable ready made wire loops, otherwise you should use the strong but thin galvanised wire and pass the ends through the cork and tie firmly. If this is not obtainable then make do with strong string or twine.

A covering of foil over the cork on a sparkling wine looks attractive and professional.

In view of the vigorous process of fermentation use heavy quality glass bottles for either a dry or sweet sparkling wine.

To bottle your wines

The look of a bottle of wine is very important when you serve it, so take trouble to bottle it as attractively as you possibly can.

Obviously you will see that the bottles are very clean on the inside.

Fill well up the neck of the bottle.

Put on the cork. If you have not got a corking machine you will have to press very firmly to make sure the cork really is sealed. Twist clean foil over the top to look like a commercial wine, seal and label very attractively. If you make a lot of wine, it is a good idea to date your bottles so that you are certain you are using the right year or vintage.

Allowing wines to mature

The time the wines will take to mature varies and an indication is given in the recipes as to the time each wine takes. It does not matter leaving them longer, but if you try to use them too soon the best flavour will not be obtained.

Using yeast

Using yeast in wine makes certain that your wine will ferment properly. It is better to use brewers' rather than bakers' yeast, since this has been formulated for the purpose of wine making.

The best yeast to use in wine making however is that specially produced for the purpose. Large chemists and some stores now have a special counter where they sell many utensils, etc., to help in making wine and also the special wine yeast. Choose this in preference to all others.

There are two ways of adding the yeast; it can either be spread on a piece of dry toast or can be added direct to the liquid.

Wine outfits

Today many Chemists have special 'quick making' wine outfits, with the juices all ready, so if you wish to make wine in the easiest possible way then try these.

Fruit Wines

Preparing fruit for wine making

Since the wine is strained so carefully, your fruit can be put in without peeling, topping and tailing or removing cores. It is imperative to see that the fruit is cleaned and that any imperfect parts are cut away, though the little flower stalks on blackcurrants, gooseberries, etc., need not be removed.

Hard fruits

Peel or slice fairly thinly in order to extract the maximum amount of juice. You will find reference made in the recipes to pressing, which again helps to remove the juice. With the exception of quinces, which are exceptionally hard, the fruit should not be cooked or allowed to become pulpy. It is for this reason that you should not grate the fruit.

Soft fruits

Select with care. Soft fruit should be ripe, but not over-ripe. Throw away any mildewed fruits or very over-ripe berries. Wash, but dry before using, or if you have left them a little damp, slightly reduce the amount of water in the recipe.

Weight of fruit

The weight of fruit is given clearly in each recipe, but if you intend to remove the stones, add a little more fruit. After your first year, you may find that you would like a slightly stronger wine in flavour, in which case increase the amount of fruit slightly, but you will find that the varying proportions of fruit, water, sugar have been designed to give the maximum of flavour to suit most palates.

Stones of fruit

You can, if wished, include the stones in plums, apricots, etc., but remember they add a slightly almond flavour to your wine.

Flavour of fruit wines

Each fruit will give its own particular flavour to the wine, but as a general guide these are the flavours you will obtain.

Apple	light white wine
Apricot	sweet white wine
Blackberry	rich red wine
Blackcurrant	port wine
Cherry	claret
Damson	very dry red wine
Elderberry	port
Gooseberry	sweet champagne
Grape	light dry white wine
Greengage	light white wine
Hips	very dry white wine
Haws	dry white wine
Lemon	very dry wine
Loganberry	vin rosé
Mulberry	very dry red wine
Nectarine	sweet white wine
Orange	light sherry
Peach	sweet white wine
Pear	light white wine
Plum	red wine
Quince	very dry white wine
Raisin	light port
Raspberry	vin rosé
Redcurrant	dry vin rosé
Rhubarb	very dry white wine
Sloe	red wine

Sparkling fruit wines

Clear wines are most popular, but if you are fond of sparkling wines the majority of your fruit wines can be produced in this way, see recipes.

Apple wine

you will need:
4 lb. apples | 8 pints boiling water

To each gallon juice:
3 lb. sugar | juice 2 lemons
½ oz. yeast

1 Cut apples into pieces—do not peel or core.
2 Pour over the water, pressing well to extract juice. Leave for 4 days to infuse.
3 Strain off the juice and measure.
4 Add sugar and yeast and lemon juice and leave to ferment (bubble) in a warm place (65°F.–75°F.).
5 When bubbling ceases, stir well.
6 Leave for a further 3 days for the sediment to settle.
7 Strain through flannel or *very thick* muslin into a cask, filling the cask completely. If wine is not clear see instructions on page 10.
8 Cork and leave for 6 months.
9 Pour into bottles, cork and store in a *cool dark* place to mature for another few months at least.

Sparkling apple wine

you will need:
4 lb. apples | 8 pints boiling water

To each gallon juice:
3 lb. sugar | juice 2 lemons
½ oz. yeast

Follow method as Apple wine, steps 1 to 4.
5 After some weeks, just before fermentation ceases (see page 12)—you will be able to judge this as the process slows down—strain into bottles. (As the wine is still working the bottles must be very strong so that they will not burst, and preferably have screw tops, or the corks should be wired down.)
6 Store in a cool place.

Dry apple wine

Recipe as Apple wine but use only 2 lb. sugar.

Sparkling dry apple wine

Follow recipe for Sparkling apple wine, but use 2 lb. sugar only.

Crab-apple wine

you will need:
4 lb. crab apples | 8 pints boiling water
To each gallon juice: | juice 2 lemons
3 lb. sugar | ½ oz. yeast

Method as for Apple wine (see left), but leave the wine for 12 months.

Sparkling crab-apple wine

Use ingredients as Crab-apple wine and follow method for Sparkling apple wine.

Cranberry and apple wine

Cranberries by themselves do not produce a wine which is palatable to many people. They are, however, very good mixed with apples. Choose ripe cranberries.

you will need:
2 lb. cranberries | 8 pints boiling water
2 lb. apples

To each gallon juice:
3 lb. sugar | ½ oz. yeast

Method as for Apple wine (see left).

Sparkling cranberry and apple wine

Use ingredients as Cranberry and apple wine, then follow instructions for Sparkling apple wine.

Apricot wine

you will need:
6 lb. apricots | 8 pints boiling water
To each gallon juice:
3 lb. sugar | ¼ oz. yeast
juice 2 lemons

1 Halve the apricots. If you like the almond flavour given by the stones, you can leave them in, or for a better result crack and leave in the kernels.
2 Pour over the water, pressing well to extract juice.
3 Leave for 4 days to infuse.
4 Strain off liquid and measure.
5 Add sugar and lemon juice and yeast and leave to ferment in a warm place (65°F.–75°F.).
6 When bubbling ceases, stir well.

7 Leave for a further 3 days for the sediment to settle.

8 Strain through flannel or *very thick* muslin into a cask, filling this completely. If wine is not clear see instructions on page 10.

9 Cork and leave for 6 months.

10 Pour into bottles, cork and store in a *cool dark* place to mature for another few months at least.

Sparkling apricot wine

Use ingredients as Apricot wine and follow instructions, steps 1 to 5. Before fermentation ceases (see Sparkling apple wine, and page 12) strain, bottle, cork and store.

Dry apricot wine

Recipe as Apricot wine but use only 2½ lb. sugar.

Sparkling dry apricot wine

Follow recipe for Sparkling apricot wine, but use 2½ lb. sugar instead of 3 lb.

Blackberry wine

you will need:
6 lb. blackberries   6 pints boiling water

To each gallon juice:
2½ lb. sugar   ¼ oz. yeast

1 Put blackberries into container.

2 Pour over boiling water, press hard to extract juice.

3 Leave 4 days to infuse.

4 Strain off liquid.

5 Measure the juice and add sugar and yeast.

6 Leave to ferment in a warm place (65°F.–75°F.).

7 When bubbling ceases (in this wine it may be only 2–3 weeks), stir well.

8 Leave for a further 3 days for the sediment to settle.

9 Strain through flannel or *very thick* muslin into a cask, filling the cask completely.

10 Cork and leave at least 4 months.

11 Pour into bottles.

12 Cork and store in a *cool dark* place to mature for another few months at least.

Sparkling blackberry wine

Use ingredients as Blackberry wine and follow method, steps 1 to 6. Bottle before fermentation ceases—see Sparkling apple wine.

Sweet blackberry wine

Recipe as Blackberry wine but increase sugar to 3–3½ lb.

Sparkling sweet blackberry wine

Use ingredients as Sparkling blackberry wine but increase sugar to 3–3½ lb. Follow method as Sparkling blackberry wine.

Blackberry and apple wine

you will need:
2 lb. apples   7 pints water
3 lb. blackberries

To each gallon juice:
2 lb. sugar   ¼ oz. yeast

1 Cut the fruit into pieces and pour over the water, pressing well to extract juice.

2 Leave for 4 days to infuse.

3 Strain off liquid and measure.

4 Add sugar and yeast and leave to ferment in a warm place (65°F.–75°F.).

5 When bubbling ceases, stir well.

6 Leave for a further 3 days for the sediment to settle.

7 Strain through flannel or *very thick* muslin into a cask, filling this completely. If wine is not clear see instructions on page 10.

8 Cork and leave for 6 months.

9 Pour into bottles, cork and store in a *cool dark* place to mature for another few months at least.

Variation

With cinnamon: add 1 stick of cinnamon to the fruit before pouring over the water.

Sparkling blackberry and apple wine

Use ingredients as Blackberry and apple wine and follow the method, steps 1 to 4. Strain, bottle and cork before fermentation ceases, see Sparkling apple wine.

Blackcurrant wine

you will need:

5 lb. blackcurrants   7 pints boiling water

To each gallon juice:
3 lb. sugar   ¼ oz. yeast

1 Put blackcurrants into container.
2 Pour over boiling water, press hard to extract juice.
3 Leave 4 days to infuse.
4 Strain off liquid.
5 Measure the juice and add sugar and yeast.
6 Leave to ferment in a warm place (65°F.–75°F.).
7 When bubbling ceases (in this wine it may be only 2–3 weeks) stir well.
8 Leave for a further 3 days for the sediment to settle.
9 Strain through flannel or *very thick* muslin into a cask, filling the cask completely.
10 Cork and leave for 7–9 months to mature.
11 Pour into bottles.
12 Cork and store in a *cool dark* place for another few months at least.

Sparkling blackcurrant wine

Use ingredients as Blackcurrant wine and follow instructions, steps 1 to 5 (fermentation may last for only 2–3 weeks) then strain, bottle and cork as Sparkling apple wine.

Dry blackcurrant wine

Recipe as Blackcurrant wine, using 2½ lb. sugar. When adding the sugar include the juice of 2 lemons.

Sparkling dry blackcurrant wine

Follow recipe for Sparkling blackcurrant wine, but use only 2½ lb. sugar, and when adding this include the juice of 2 lemons.

Black and redcurrant wine

2½ lb. blackcurrants   7 pints boiling water
2½ lb. redcurrants

To each gallon juice:
3 lb. sugar   ¼ oz. yeast

Method as for Blackcurrant wine.

Sparkling black and redcurrant wine

Use ingredients as Black and redcurrant wine and follow instructions for Sparkling blackcurrant wine.

Blueberry wine (or whortleberry, blaeberry, bilberry)

you will need:

4 lb. blueberries   few rosemary leaves
4 pints water   4 pints draught cider
½ oz. cream of tartar   when bottling
½ oz. root ginger

To each gallon juice:
2½ lb. sugar   ¼ oz. yeast

1 Put blueberries into container.
2 Pour over boiling water, press hard to extract juice.
3 Add the cream of tartar, ginger and the bruised rosemary leaves.
4 Leave 4 days to infuse, and strain off liquid.
5 Measure the juice and add sugar and yeast.
6 Leave to ferment in a warm place (65°F.–75°F.).
7 When bubbling ceases (in this wine it may be only 2–3 weeks) stir well.
8 Leave for a further 3 days for the sediment to settle.
9 Strain through flannel or *very thick* muslin into a cask, filling the cask completely.
10 Cork and leave for 7–9 months to mature.
11 Strain and blend with the draught cider and pour into bottles.
12 Cork and store in a *cool dark* place for another few months at least.

Sparkling blueberry wine

Use ingredients as Blueberry wine and follow method for clear wine, steps 1 to 6. Before bubbling ceases (with this wine fermentation may last only 2–3 weeks), strain, bottle and cork as Sparkling apple wine.

Cherry plum wine

you will need:

7 lb. cherry plums	1 gallon boiling water

To each gallon juice:

3 lb. sugar	juice 2 lemons
¼ oz. yeast	

1 Put plums into container and pour over boiling water. If plums are firm you need to press very hard to extract juice.
2 Leave for 4 days to infuse.
3 Strain off liquid and measure.
4 Add sugar, yeast and lemon juice and leave to ferment in a warm place (65°F.–75°F.).
5 When bubbling ceases (in this wine it may be only 2–3 weeks), stir well.
6 Leave for a further 3 days for the sediment to settle.
7 Strain through flannel or *very thick* muslin into a cask, filling the cask completely.
8 Cork and leave for at least 5 months.
9 Pour into bottles.
10 Cork and store in a *cool dark* place to mature for another few months at least.

Sparkling cherry plum wine

Use ingredients as Cherry plum wine and follow the method, steps 1 to 4. This wine may ferment for only 2–3 weeks, and before bubbling ceases, strain, bottle and cork as Sparkling apple wine.

Morello cherry wine (1)

you will need:

7 lb. morello cherries	1 gallon boiling water

To each gallon juice:

3 lb. sugar	¼ oz. yeast

1 Put cherries into container and pour over boiling water. If cherries are firm you need to press very hard to extract juice.
2 Leave for 4 days to infuse.
3 Strain off liquid and measure.
4 Add sugar and yeast and leave to ferment in a warm place (65°F.–75°F.).
5 When bubbling ceases (in this wine it may be only 2–3 weeks), stir well.
6 Leave for a further 3 days for the sediment to settle.
7 Strain through flannel or *very thick* muslin into a cask, filling the cask completely.
8 Cork and leave for at least 5 months.
9 Pour into bottles.
10 Cork and store in a *cool dark* place to mature for another few months at least.

Note

This is one of the very few fruits where it is possible to use the cherries in pies. They have a slightly winey flavour.

Sparkling morello cherry wine

Use ingredients as for Morello cherry wine (1) and follow the method, steps 1 to 4. Before fermentation ceases, and in the case of this wine it may be only 2–3 weeks, strain, bottle and cork as Sparkling apple wine.

Morello cherry wine (2)

you will need:

7 lb. morello cherries	1 pint ale when
6 pints water	bottling

To each gallon juice:

3 lb. sugar	¼ oz. yeast

1 Put cherries into container and pour over boiling water. If cherries are firm you need to press very hard to extract juice.
2 Leave for 4 days to infuse.
3 Strain off liquid and measure.
4 Add sugar and yeast and leave to ferment in a warm place (65°F.–75°F.).
5 When bubbling ceases, stir well.
6 Leave for a further 3 days for the sediment to settle.
7 Strain through flannel or *very thick* muslin into a cask, filling the cask completely.
8 Cork and leave for at least 5 months.
9 Blend with the ale and pour into bottles.
10 Cork and store in a *cool dark* place to mature for another few months at least.

Black cherry wine

Recipe as Morello cherry wine using only 2½ lb. sugar.

Sparkling black cherry wine

Use black cherries and ingredients as Morello cherry wine (1) but 2½ lb. sugar only. Follow method for Sparkling morello cherry wine.

White cherry wine

Recipe as Morello cherry wine but add a little port wine before storing (point 10) to give flavour and colour.

Sparkling white cherry wine

Using ingredients as for Morello cherry wine, with white cherries, follow method for Sparkling morello cherry wine, but add a little port wine to give colour and flavour, before bottling.

Dry morello cherry wine

Recipe as Morello cherry wine, but use only 2 lb. sugar and the juice of 1 lemon to each gallon of juice.

Sparkling dry morello cherry wine

Use ingredients and follow method as for Sparkling morello cherry wine, but add only 2 lb. sugar and the juice of 1 lemon to each gallon of juice.

Damson wine

you will need:

4 lb. ripe damsons   1 gallon water

To each gallon juice:
3 lb. sugar   ¼ oz. yeast

1 Put the fruit into container and pour over the boiling water, pressing well to extract juice. Even ripe damsons tend to be very firm, so they must be pressed well.
3 Leave for 4 days to infuse.
3 Strain off liquid and measure.
4 Add sugar and yeast and leave to ferment in a warm place (65°F.–75°F.).
5 When bubbling ceases, stir well.
6 Leave for a further 3 days for the sediment to settle.

7 Strain through flannel or *very thick* muslin into a cask, filling this completely. If wine is not clear see instructions on page 10.
8 Cork and leave for 6 months.
9 Pour into bottles, cork and store in a *cool dark* place to mature for another few months at least.

Variation

With ginger: add ½ oz. root ginger and juice of 1 lemon with the sugar.

Sparkling damson wine

Use ingredients as Damson wine and follow the method steps 1 to 4. Before fermentation ceases, strain, bottle and cork as Sparkling apple wine.

Damson and greengage wine

you will need:

2 lb. ripe damsons   1 gallon water
2 lb. greengages

To each gallon juice:
3 lb. sugar   ¼ oz. yeast

Method as for Damson wine.

Sparkling damson and greengage wine

Use ingredients as Damson and greengage wine, and follow method as for Sparkling damson wine.

Elderberry wine

you will need:

4 lb. elderberries   9 pints boiling water

To each gallon juice:
2½ lb. sugar   ¼ oz. root ginger
¼ oz. yeast   8 oz. raisins

Method as for Rhubarb wine (see page 26). but flavour with root ginger and raisins.

Sparkling elderberry wine

This makes a particularly good sparkling wine. Use ingredients as Elderberry wine and follow instructions for Sparkling rhubarb wine (see page 27).

Sweet elderberry wine

Method and ingredients as Elderberry wine but use 3¼ lb. sugar.

Sparkling sweet elderberry wine

Use ingredients as Elderberry wine but add 3¼ lb. sugar. Follow the method for Sparkling rhubarb wine (see page 27).

Gooseberry wine (1)

you will need:

4 lb. fruit (use green gooseberries)   9 pints boiling water

To each gallon juice:
3 lb. sugar   1 oz. ginger
¼ oz. yeast

Method as for Rhubarb wine (see page 26).

Sparkling gooseberry wine

This also makes a specially good sparkling wine. Use ingredients as Gooseberry wine (1) and follow the instructions for Sparkling rhubarb wine (see page 27).

Gooseberry wine (2)

Method as for Gooseberry wine (1), but add 1 pint brandy. This is a particularly potent wine and an excellent one to store.

Dry gooseberry wine

Method and ingredients as above, but use only 2½ lb. sugar.

Sparkling dry gooseberry wine

Use ingredients as Gooseberry wine (1) but only 2½ lb. sugar. Follow the method given for Sparkling rhubarb wine (see page 27).

Grape wines

There are a number of recipes below for making grape wines.

The choice of grapes makes a vast difference to the colour and flavour of your wine. The dark grapes will give you an attractive pink wine.

Grape wine

you will need:

4 lb. grapes (black if possible)   5 pints boiling water

To each gallon juice:
2 lb. sugar   1 teaspoon almond essence
¼ oz. yeast

1 Put the fruit into a container and pour over the water, pressing well to extract juice.
2 Leave for 4 days to infuse.
3 Strain off liquid and measure.
4 Add sugar, yeast and almond essence and leave to ferment in a warm place (65°F.–75°F.).
5 When bubbling ceases, stir well.
6 Strain for a further 3 days for the sediment to settle.
7 Strain through flannel or *very thick* muslin into a cask, filling this completely. If wine is not clear, see instructions on page 10.
8 Cork and leave for 6 months.
9 Pour into bottles, cork and store in a *cool dark* place to mature for another few months at least.

Note
This is a very dry grape wine.

Sparkling dry grape wine

Use ingredients as Grape wine and follow the method, steps 1 to 4. Bottle before fermentation ceases, see Sparkling apple wine.

Sweet grape wine (1)

Ingredients as Grape wine but increase sugar to 3 lb.

Sparkling sweet grape wine

Use ingredients as either Sweet grape wine (1) or (2), and follow the method for Sparkling grape wine.

Sweet grape wine (2)

you will need:

4 lb. grapes (white if possible)   1 gallon water

To each gallon juice:
3½–4½ lb. sugar   ¼ oz. yeast

Method as for Grape wine (1).

Grape and raisin wine

Use any of the recipes for Grape wine, but add 8 oz. dried raisins to the fruit.

Sparkling grape and raisin wine

Use ingredients as for either Grape wine, but add 8 oz. dried raisins to the fruit. Follow the method as for Sparkling dry grape wine.

Grapefruit wine

you will need:

3 large grapefruit   1 gallon water

To each gallon juice:
3 lb. sugar   ½ oz. yeast

Method as for Lemon wine (see page 21).

Sparkling grapefruit wine

Use ingredients as for Grapefruit wine but follow the method for Sparkling lemon wine (see page 21).

Greengage wine

you will need:

5 lb. greengages   pared rind 2 lemons
8 pints boiling water

To each gallon juice:
2–2½ lb. sugar   juice 1 orange
¼ oz. yeast

1 Cut the fruit into halves and pour over the boiling water, adding the lemon rind.
2 Press well to extract juice and leave for 4 days to infuse.
3 Strain off liquid and measure.
4 Add sugar, juice and yeast and leave to ferment in a warm place (65°F.–75°F.).
5 When bubbling ceases, stir well.

6 Leave for a further 3 days for the sediment to settle.
7 Strain through flannel of *very thick* muslin into a cask, filling this completely. If wine is not clear, see instructions on page 10.
8 Cork and leave for 6 months.
9 Pour into bottles, cork and store in a *cool dark* place to mature for another few months at least.

Sparkling greengage wine

Use ingredients as Greengage wine and follow the method, steps 1 to 4. Before fermentation ceases, strain, bottle and cork as Sparkling apple wine.

Hip wine (1)

you will need:

6 lb. hips   6 pints boiling water

To each gallon juice:
2½ lb. sugar   ¼ oz. yeast

1 Put hips into container and pour over boiling water.
2 As hips are very hard you need to leave them for approximately 1 week, pressing very hard every day.
3 Strain off liquid.
4 Measure the juice and add sugar and yeast.
5 Leave in a warm place (65°F.–75°F.) to ferment.
6 When bubbling ceases, stir well.
7 Leave for a further 3 days for the sediment to settle.
8 Strain through flannel or *very thick* muslin into a cask.
9 Fill the cask completely, cork and leave at least 4 months.
10 Pour into bottles, cork and store in a *cool dark* place to mature for another few months at least.

Sparkling hip wine

Use ingredients as Hip wine and follow the method, steps 1 to 5. Proceed to strain, bottle and cork as Sparkling apple wine.

Rose hip wine

you will need:

4 lb. rose hips
1 gallon boiling water
1 oz. citric acid or juice 3 lemons

To each gallon juice:
3 lb. sugar
¼ oz. yeast

1 Gather the rose hips after the first frost.
2 Cut in half or mince.
3 Put rose hips, sugar and citric acid or lemon juice into a large bowl.
4 Pour over boiling water.
5 Stir well.
6 When mixture is lukewarm add yeast.
7 Cover well.
8 Leave until fermentation ceases—this may be shorter than in some wines.
9 Strain into cask.
10 Proceed as for Rhubarb wine (see page 26).

Note

This wine has a slightly different flavour from Hip wine because citric acid or lemons are used.

Although lemons give a bite to this wine, it can be made dryer by using only 2¼ lb. sugar.

Sparkling rose hip wine

Use ingredients as for Rose hip wine and follow the method, steps 1 to 7. Leave to ferment—this process may not be as long as for some wines—and before bubbling ceases, strain, bottle and cork as for Sparkling apple wine.

Haw wine

you will need:

6 lb. haws
6 pints boiling water

To each gallon juice:
2½ lb. sugar
¼ oz. yeast

Method as for Hip wine.

Sparkling haw wine

Use ingredients as Haw wine and follow the method for Sparkling hip wine.

Lemon wine

you will need:

12 large lemons
1 gallon water

To each gallon juice:
3 lb. sugar
½ oz. yeast

1 Slice the lemons.
2 Pour over the boiling water and leave for 3 days to infuse.
3 Strain off liquid and measure.
4 Add sugar and yeast and leave to ferment in a warm place (65°F.–75°F.).
5 When bubbling ceases, stir well.
6 Leave for a further 3 days for the sediment to settle.
7 Strain through flannel or *very thick* muslin into a cask, filling this completely. If wine is not clear see instructions on page 10.
8 Cork and leave for 12 months.
9 Pour into bottles, cork and store in a *cool dark* place to mature for another few months at least.

Sparkling lemon wine

Use ingredients as Lemon wine, and follow the instructions, steps 1 to 4. Before fermentation ceases, strain, bottle and cork as Sparkling apple wine.

Dry lemon wine

Although lemon can be made into a dry wine, it will be very much a matter of personal taste because of the acidity of the lemons.

Method and ingredients as Lemon wine but use only 2½ lb. sugar.

Sparkling dry lemon wine

Use ingredients as Lemon wine, but only 2½ lb. sugar. Follow instructions as for Sparkling lemon wine.

Lime wine

Limes do not make a very pleasant wine by themselves but 1 or 2 limes can be mixed with lemons.

Sparkling lemon and lime wine

Use ingredients as Lemon wine, mixing 1 or 2 limes with lemons. Follow method as Sparkling lemon wine.

Loganberry wine

you will need:

6 lb. loganberries   1 gallon boiling water

To each gallon juice:
2½ lb. sugar   ¼ oz. yeast

1 Put fruit into container and pour over the water.
2 Mash firmly, pressing well to extract juice and leave for 4 days to infuse.
3 Strain off liquid and measure.
4 Add sugar and yeast and leave in a warm place (65°F.–75°F.) to ferment.
5 When bubbling ceases, stir well.
6 Leave for a further 3 days for the sediment to settle.
7 Strain through flannel or *very thick* muslin into a cask, filling this completely. If wine is not clear see instructions on page 10.
8 Cork and leave for 6 months.
9 Pour into bottles, cork and store in a *cool dark* place to mature for another few months at least.

Sparkling loganberry wine

Use ingredients as Loganberry wine and follow method, steps 1 to 4. Before bubbling ceases, strain, bottle and cork as Sparkling apple wine.

Sweet loganberry wine

Recipe as Loganberry wine, but use 3 lb. sugar.

Sparkling sweet loganberry wine

Use ingredients as Loganberry wine, but 3 lb. sugar. Follow the method for Sparkling loganberry wine.

Mixed fruit wines

For a mixed fruit wine one obviously chooses those fruits that blend well together. In this book there are a number of wines where two types of fruit have been mixed together as in the following recipes.

Raspberries and redcurrants

Use 1 lb. mixed fruit and make as Raspberry wine (see page 26).

Sparkling raspberry and redcurrant wine

Use 1 lb. mixed fruit and make as Sparkling raspberry wine (see page 26).

Damson and plum

Make as Damson wine (see page 18) using 1 lb. mixed fruit.

Sparkling damson and plum wine

Make as Sparkling damson wine (see page 18) using 1 lb. mixed fruit.

Rhubarb and raspberry

An excellent way to eke out expensive raspberries. Use 1 lb. mixed fruit and make as Rhubarb wine (see page 26).

Sparkling rhubarb and raspberry wine

Use 1 lb. mixed fruit and make as Sparkling rhubarb wine.

Cherry and apricot

Make as Morello cherry wine (see page 17), using 1 lb. mixed fruit.

Sparkling cherry and apricot wine

Use 1 lb. mixed fruit and make as Sparkling morello cherry wine (see page 17).

Mulberry wine

you will need:

6 lb. mulberries	1 gallon boiling water

To each gallon juice:

2½ lb. sugar	¼ oz. yeast

Method as for Loganberry wine.

Variations

With cinnamon: add a stick of cinnamon to the fruit and continue as for loganberry wine.

With brandy: to each gallon of juice allow ½ pint brandy and keep 12 months to mature.

Sparkling mulberry wine

Use ingredients as Mulberry wine and follow the method for Sparkling loganberry wine (see page 22).

Nectarine wine

you will need:

6 lb. nectarines	8 pints boiling water

To each gallon juice:

3 lb. sugar	½ oz. yeast
juice 3 lemons	

1 Halve the nectarines.
2 Pour over the water, pressing well to extract juice.
3 Leave for 4 days to infuse.
4 Strain off liquid and measure.
5 Add sugar, lemon juice and yeast and leave to ferment in a warm place (65°F.–75°F.).
6 When bubbling ceases, stir well.
7 Leave for a further 3 days for the sediment to settle.
8 Strain through flannel or *very thick* muslin into a cask, filling this completely. If wine is not clear see instructions on page 10.
9 Cork and leave for 6 months.
10 Pour into bottles, cork and store in a *cool dark* place to mature for another few months at least.

Sparkling nectarine wine

Use ingredients as Nectarine wine and follow the method, steps 1 to 5. Strain, bottle and cork as Sparkling apple wine (see page 14).

Orange wine (1)

you will need:

6 lb. oranges	8 pints boiling water

To each gallon juice:

juice 2 lemons	3 lb. sugar
¼ oz. yeast	

Method as for Rhubarb wine (see page 26) but spread the yeast over toast when adding to the juice.

Sparkling orange wine (1)

Use ingredients as Orange wine (1) and follow the method for Sparkling rhubarb wine—spreading the yeast over toast when adding to the juice.

Orange wine (2)

you will need:

14 oranges	1 gallon water

To each gallon juice:

3 lb. sugar	½ oz. yeast

Method as for Lemon wine (see page 21). The pips give a slightly less sweet flavour so can be removed before making the wine.

Orange and raisin wine

As either recipe for Orange wine, but add 8 oz. raisins to the fruit and continue as before.

Sparkling orange wine (2)

Use ingredients as Orange wine (2) and follow the instructions for Sparkling lemon wine (see page 21).

Sparkling orange and raisin wine

Use either of the recipes for Orange wine, but add 8 oz. raisins to fruit, and follow the instructions for Sparkling orange wine (1).

Dry orange wine

Ingredients and method as for Orange wine (1) but use only 2¼ lb. sugar.

Sparkling dry orange wine

Use ingredients and follow instructions as for Sparkling orange wine (1) but use only 2¼ lb. sugar.

Peach wine

you will need:

6 lb. peaches   8 pints boiling water

To each gallon juice:
3 lb. sugar   ¼ oz. yeast
juice 2 lemons

Method as for Apricot wine (see page 14).

Sparkling peach wine

Use ingredients as for Peach wine and follow method for Sparkling apricot wine (see page 15).

Pear wine

you will need:

4 lb. pears   8 pints boiling water

To each gallon juice:
3 lb. sugar   ¼ oz. yeast
juice 2 lemons

Method as for Apple wine (see page 14).

You can use the very hard pears that are not good enough for perry.
You will need to press hard, but you should not have to cook as with quinces.
This wine matures quickly so can be used after 3 months.

Sparkling pear wine

Use ingredients as Pear wine, and follow the instructions for Sparkling apple wine (see page 14)

Plum wine

you will need:
4 lb. ripe plums*   5 pints boiling water
1 lb. sugar

To each gallon juice:
1½ lb. sugar   ¼ oz. yeast
* By using a different type of plum with each lot of wine you produce a good variety of flavours.

1 Sprinkle sugar over halved plums.
2 Add boiling water.
3 Proceed as for Rhubarb wine (see page 26) but add the cracked plum stones to the juice together with the sugar and yeast.

Sparkling plum wine

Use ingredients as for Plum wine and follow the method, steps 1 and 2. Then proceed as Sparkling rhubarb wine (see page 27).

Dry plum wine

A Victoria plum does not produce a good dry wine. However, some of the smaller red plums give an excellent result.
Sprinkle the sugar over the plums as recommended above, but add only 1 lb. sugar and the juice of 1 lemon to each gallon of juice.

Sparkling dry plum wine

Use small red plums and the other ingredients as Plum wine. Sprinkle sugar over halved plums but add 1 lb. sugar and the juice of 1 lemon to each gallon juice. Follow instructions for Sparkling rhubarb wine.

Quince wine

you will need:

6 lb. quinces	8 pints boiling water

To each gallon juice:

juice and grated rind 3 lemons	2½ lb. sugar ¼ oz. yeast

1 Since quinces are so hard, you will need to grate or chop them very finely leaving the core.
2 Because the quinces are so hard, pouring over the boiling water is not sufficient. Put into a pan and simmer for approximately 15 minutes, pressing the fruit down hard. It should, however, not be allowed to become a pulp, otherwise your wine will never be clear.
3 Leave for 4 days to infuse.
4 Strain off liquid, and measure.
5 Add juice and rind of lemons, sugar and yeast and leave in a warm place (65°F.–75°F.) to ferment.
6 When bubbling ceases, stir well.
7 Leave for a further 3 days for the sediment to settle.
8 Strain through flannel or *very thick* muslin into a cask. The cask must be completely filled, otherwise your wine will taste like vinegar. If wine is not clear see instructions on page 10.
9 Cork and leave for 6 months.
10 Pour into bottles, cork and store in a *cool dark* place to mature for another few months at least.

Sparkling quince wine

Use ingredients as Quince wine and follow the instructions, steps 1 to 5. Before bubbling ceases, strain, bottle and cork as Sparkling apple wine.

Quince and apple wine

you will need:

3 lb. quinces 2 lb. apples	8 pints boiling water

To each gallon juice:

2½ lb. sugar ¼ oz. yeast	juice and grated rind 2 lemons

Method as for Quince wine above, but simmer the quinces only and after 15 minutes add the chopped apples.

Sparkling quince and apple wine

Use ingredients as for Quince and apple wine and follow the method, steps 1 to 5, but simmer quinces only and after 15 minutes add the chopped apples. Continue as Sparkling apple wine.

Raisin wine

you will need:

4 lb. dried raisins 7 pints boiling water	2 sliced oranges

To each gallon juice:

2 lb. sugar	¼ oz. yeast

Method as for Rhubarb wine (see page 26).

Sparkling raisin wine

Use ingredients as raisin wine and follow instructions for Sparkling rhubarb wine (see page 27).

Dry raisin wine

Raisin wine does tend to be a fairly medium wine and it is not particularly suitable to add less sugar for fermentation purposes, but lemons can be used in place of oranges to give a slightly dryer taste.

Sparkling dry raisin wine

Use ingredients as Raisin wine, substituting lemons for oranges, and follow the method as for Sparkling rhubarb wine.

Tea wine

you will need:

2 pints tea 2–4 oz. raisins	1 lb. sugar juice 1 lemon

1 Make the tea in the usual way, but leave the water over the tea leaves for at least 2 weeks, adding the other ingredients.
2 Allow to mature for several months.
3 This can either be served as a wine by itself or as an accompaniment to gin.

Raspberry wine (1)

you will need:

6 lb. raspberries   1 gallon boiling water

To each gallon juice:
2½ lb. sugar   ¼ oz. yeast

Method as for Rhubarb wine (see page 26) but after pouring water over fruit mash firmly and leave for 4 days.

Sparkling raspberry wine

Use ingredients as Raspberry wine (1), pouring boiling water over fruit, then mashing firmly and leaving for 4 days. Thereafter follow the method for Sparkling rhubarb wine.

Sweet raspberry wine

Ingredients as above, but use 3 lb. sugar.

Sparkling sweet raspberry wine

Use ingredients as Sparkling raspberry wine, but add 3 lb. sugar and follow same method.

Redcurrant wine

you will need:

6 lb. redcurrants   8 pints water

To each gallon juice:
3 lb. sugar   ¼ oz. yeast

1 Put redcurrants into container.
2 Pour over boiling water, press hard to extract juice.
3 Leave 4 days to infuse.
4 Strain off liquid.
5 Measure the juice and add sugar and yeast.
6 Leave to ferment in a warm place (65°F.–75°F.).
7 When bubbling ceases (in this wine it may be only 2–3 weeks), stir well.
8 Leave for a further 3 days for the sediment to settle.
9 Strain through flannel or *very thick* muslin into a cask, filling the cask completely.
10 Cork and leave for at least 10 months to mature.
11 Pour into bottles.
12 Cork and store in a *cool dark* place for another few months at least.

Sparkling redcurrant wine

Use ingredients as Redcurrant wine and follow the method, steps 1 to 6. Before fermentation ceases (in this case possibly only 2–3 weeks), strain, bottle and cork as Sparkling apple wine.

Dry redcurrant wine

Ingredients as above but use only 2¼ lb. sugar. This is really a rather dry wine and is very much a matter of personal taste.

Sparkling dry redcurrant wine

Use ingredients as Redcurrant wine, but only 2¼ lb. sugar and follow the instructions, steps 1 to 6. Before bubbles cease (in this case it may be only a 2–3 week fermentation period), strain, bottle and cork as Sparkling apple wine.

Whitecurrant wine

Recipe as for Redcurrant wine above using whitecurrants instead of redcurrants.

Sparkling whitecurrant wine

Use ingredients as Sparkling redcurrant wine, but whitecurrants. Follow the method for Sparkling redcurrant wine.

Rhubarb wine

you will need:

4 lb. rhubarb   6 pints boiling water

To each gallon juice:
2½ lb. sugar   juice ½ lemon
¼ oz. yeast   juice ½ orange

1 Cut the fruit into pieces and pour over the water, pressing well to extract juice.
2 Leave for 4 days to infuse.
3 Strain off liquid and measure.
4 Add sugar and yeast (which can be spread on a small piece of toast or mixed with a little of the liquid).

5 Add fruit juice and leave to ferment in a warm place (65°F.–75°F.).
6 When bubbling ceases (this will be after 4–6 weeks), stir well.
7 Leave for a further 3 days for the sediment to settle.
8 Strain through flannel or *very thick* muslin into a cask. The cask must be completely filled, otherwise your wine will taste like vinegar. If wine is not clear see instructions on page 10.
9 Cork and leave for 6 months.
10 Pour into bottles, cork and store in a *cool dark* place to mature for another few months at least.

Sparkling rhubarb wine

you will need:

4 lb. rhubarb   6 pints boiling water

To each gallon juice:
2½ lb. sugar   juice ½ lemon
¼ oz. yeast   juice ½ orange

1 Cut the fruit into pieces and pour over the water, pressing well to extract juice.
2 Leave for 4 days to infuse.
3 Strain off liquid and measure.
4 Add sugar and yeast (which can be spread on a small piece of toast or mixed with a little of the liquid).
5 Add fruit juice and leave to ferment in a warm place (65°F.–75°F.).
6 After several weeks (4–6) and before fermentation ceases, strain, bottle and cork (see page 12, and recipe for Sparkling apple wine).

Sweet rhubarb wine

As recipe for Rhubarb wine, but use 3¼ lb. sugar.

Sparkling sweet rhubarb wine

Use ingredients and follow instructions as for Sparkling rhubarb wine, but use 3¼ lb. sugar.

Rhubarb and apple wine

you will need:
3 lb. rhubarb   8 pints water
2 lb. apples

To each gallon juice:
3 lb. sugar   ¼ oz. yeast

1 Cut the fruit into pieces.
2 Pour over the water.
3 Leave for 4 days to infuse.
4 Strain off liquid.
5 Measure juice and add sugar and yeast.
6 Leave in a warm place (65°F.–75°F.) to ferment.
7 When bubbling ceases (this will be after 4–6 weeks), stir well.
8 Leave for a further 3 days for the sediment to settle.
9 Strain through flannel or *very thick* muslin into a cask. The cask must be completely filled.
10 Cork and leave for 7–8 months.
11 Pour into bottles, cork and store in a *cool dark* place to mature for another few months at least.

Sparkling rhubarb and apple wine

Use ingredients as Rhubarb and apple wine and follow method, steps 1 to 6. Before bubbling ceases, strain, bottle and cork, as Sparkling apple wine.

Dry rhubarb and apple wine

Follow the recipe for Rhubarb and apple wine, but use only 2½ lb. sugar to each gallon juice.

Sparkling dry rhubarb and apple wine

Use ingredients as Rhubarb and apple wine, but only 2½ lb. sugar. Follow instructions as for Sparkling rhubarb and apple wine.

Sloe wine

you will need:
4 lb. sloes   5 pints boiling water

To each gallon juice:
3 lb. sugar   ¼ oz. yeast

Method as for Rhubarb wine. A little brandy may be added when fermenting has ceased.

Sparkling sloe wine

Sloes make a very good sparkling wine. Use ingredients as Sloe wine and follow method as for Sparkling rhubarb wine. A little brandy may be added before bottling.

Dry sloe wine

Because sloes have a very definitely bitter flavour, you cannot produce a good dry wine with very little sugar. The minimum amount the sugar can be cut to is 2¾ lb. for each gallon juice.

Ginger wine

you will need:

4 oz. raisins	4 oz. whole ginger
3 gallons cold water	4 lemons
9 lb. loaf sugar	¼ oz. yeast

1 Stone and halve the raisins.
2 Put into a large preserving pan with the water, sugar and ginger (bruised).
3 Boil for 1 hour, skimming frequently.
4 Add the rind of the lemons.
5 Turn into a large earthenware bowl or wooden tub.
6 Allow the liquid to stand until lukewarm.
7 Add the yeast.
8 On the following day put into a clean dry cask.
9 Add the fruit of the lemons and bung lightly.
10 Stir the wine every day for a fortnight.
11 Then tighten the bung.
12 Let the wine remain undisturbed for 3–4 months, when it may be bottled for use.

Vegetable Wines

Preparing vegetables

It is unnecessary to peel vegetables since there is an appreciable amount of flavour in the skins. Vegetables should be well washed and any bruised or imperfect parts cut away. As with fruit, you slice or chop in order to extract the maximum amount of juice and you will have to press firmly.

When buying vegetables for wine, choose high quality vegetables for a poor product will not produce the flavour and clarity of wine. It is best to make your vegetable wine when vegetables are well in season. Very young vegetables do not have sufficient flavour.

Flavour of vegetable wines

Beetroot . . . rather potent, like port wine

Carrot . . . . dry sherry
Celery . . . . white wine
Marrow . dry rather flavourless white wine
Parsnip . . . . white wine
Pea . . . . . rather strong white wine
Potato . . . dry rather potent white wine
—or in some cases like brandy
Swede . . . . . . dry golden white wine
Tomato. . . . . vin rosé
Turnip . . . dry rather potent white wine

Making sweet vegetable wines

It is not particularly suitable to increase the amount of sugar since you do not have the acid bite of fruit and if too much sugar is added in a vegetable wine it is simply sickly and insipid.

Beetroot wine (1)

you will need:

4 lb. uncooked beetroot	6 pints boiling water
	2 oz. root ginger

To each gallon juice:

2 lb. sugar	juice 2 lemons
½ oz. yeast	

1 Wash and slice the beetroot.
2 Pour the boiling water over the beetroot and add the ginger.
3 Leave for 4 days to infuse.
4 Measure the liquid and add sugar, yeast and the lemon juice.
5 Leave to ferment in a warm place (65°F.–75°F.).
6 When bubbling has ceased the wine should be stirred.
7 Leave for a further 3 days to settle.
8 Strain through flannel or *very thick* muslin into a cask, cork and leave for 8–9 months.
9 Pour into bottles, if not clear, follow instructions on page 10 before bottling.
0 Cork and store in a *cool dark* place.

Beetroot wine (2)

Recipe as above, but add 12 cloves at stage 2 and when bottling add a little brandy.

Beetroot wine (3)

Recipe as for Beetroot wine (1), but use 3 lb. brown sugar and add 6-8 cloves and a small stick of cinnamon to the beetroot.

Sparkling beetroot wine

Use ingredients as either Beetroot wine (1) (2) or (3).

1 Wash and slice the beetroot.
2 Pour boiling water over and add the ginger.
3 Leave for 4 days to infuse.
4 Measure the liquid and add sugar, yeast and lemon juice.
5 Leave to ferment in a warm place (65°F.–75°F.) for several weeks.
6 Before bubbling ceases, strain, bottle and cork, wiring corks down very firmly (see page 12).

Carrot wine (1)

you will need:

4 lb. carrots	7 pints water

To each gallon juice:

2–2½ lb. sugar*	½ oz. yeast
juice 1 lemon	1 slice toast
juice 1 orange	

* Carrots are naturally sweet and for many people 2 lb. sugar is sufficient.

1 Wash and slice the carrots.
2 Pour the boiling water over them.
3 Leave for 4 days to infuse.
4 Measure the liquid and add sugar, lemon and orange juice and the yeast spread on toast.
5 Leave in a warm place (65°F.–75°F.) to ferment.
6 When bubbling has ceased the wine should be stirred.
7 Leave for 3 days to settle.
8 Strain through flannel or *very thick* muslin into a cask, cork and leave for 8 months to mature.
9 Pour into bottles, if not clear follow instructions on page 10 before bottling.
10 Cork and store in a *cool dark* place.

Carrot wine (2)

you will need:

4 lb. carrots	6 pints boiling water

To each gallon juice:

2 lb. sugar	2 oz. ginger
juice 2 lemons	½ oz. yeast

Method as for Potato wine (1) (see page 31).

Sparkling carrot wine

Use ingredients as either Carrot wine (1) or (2) and follow instructions given until fermentation has almost ceased, then strain, bottle and cork as Sparkling apple wine.

Spiced carrot wine

As recipe (1) above, but use 3 lb. demerara sugar and add about 8 cloves to the carrots when adding water.

Sparkling spiced carrot wine

Use ingredients as Carrot wine (1) but add 3 lb. demerara sugar and about 8 cloves to the carrots when adding water. Follow method, steps 1 to 5. Before bubbling ceases, strain, bottle and cork as Sparkling apple wine.

Celery wine (1)

you will need:

5 lb. celery   8 pints water

To each gallon juice:
3 lb. sugar   ½ oz. yeast
juice 1 lemon   1 oz. ginger
juice 2 oranges

1 Wash and slice the celery.
2 Pour the poiling water over and leave for 4 days to infuse.
3 Measure the liquid and add sugar, fruit juice, yeast and ginger.
4 Leave in a warm place (65°F.–75°F.) to ferment.
5 When bubbling has ceased the wine should be stirred.
6 Leave for a further 3 days to settle.
7 Strain through flannel or *very thick* muslin into a cask, cork and leave for 10–12 months.
8 Pour into bottles, if not clear follow instructions on page 10 before bottling.
9 Cork and store in a *cool dark* place.

Celery wine (2)

you will need:

5 lb. celery   8 pints water

To each gallon juice:
3 lb. sugar   juice 2 oranges
juice 3 lemons   ½ oz. yeast

Method as for Celery wine (1) see above.

Sparkling celery wine

Use ingredients as Celery wine (1) or (2) and follow method, steps 1 to 4. Before fermentation ceases, strain, bottle and cork as Sparkling apple wine.

Mango wine (1)

you will need:

4 lb. mangoes   6 pints water
1½ oz. ginger

To each gallon juice:
8 oz. pearl barley   juice 1 orange
½ oz. yeast   4 oz. raisins
juice 1 lemon   3 lb. sugar

Method as for Parsnip wine (1).

Mango wine (2)

Method as for Parsnip wine (2).

Sparkling mango wine

Use ingredients as Mango wine (1) or (2)—using 3 lb. demerara sugar and adding 6 cloves—and follow instructions for Parsnip wine (1), steps 1 to 5. Before fermentation ceases, strain, bottle and cork as Sparkling apple wine.

Marrow wine

you will need:

1 6 lb. marrow   1 gallon water
1–2 oz. root ginger

To each gallon juice:
3 lb. sugar   ½ oz. yeast
juice 3 lemons

1 Use the whole of the marrow—peel, seeds, etc.
2 Chop very finely and add the ginger and boiling water.
3 Leave for 6 days, pressing hard each day.
4 Measure the liquid and add sugar, lemon juice and yeast.
5 Leave in a warm place (65°F.–75°F.) to ferment.
6 When bubbling has ceased the wine should be stirred.
7 Leave for a further 3 days to settle.
8 Strain through flannel or *very thick* muslin into a cask, cork and leave for 6 months.
9 Pour into bottles, if not clear follow instructions on page 10 before bottling.
10 Cork and store in a *cool dark* place.

Sparkling marrow wine

Use ingredients as Marrow wine and follow the instructions, steps 1 to 5. Before bubbling subsides completely, strain, bottle and cork as Sparkling apple wine.

Parsnip wines

Many country people think that you should not use parsnips until there has been a frost. Parsnips are inclined to develop a particular bacteria, so in either of the following recipes you are wise to use 3 Campden tablets (obtainable from chemists) to each gallon of boiling water. Crush these and mix with ¼ oz. citric acid and stir into the boiling water.

Parsnip wine (1)

you will need:

4 lb. parsnips	1½ oz. ginger
6 pints water	

To each gallon juice:

3 lb. sugar	1 slice toast
4 oz. raisins	juice 1 lemon
8 oz. pearl barley	juice 1 orange
½ oz. yeast	

1 Wash and slice the parsnips.
2 Pour the boiling water over them, adding the ginger.
3 Leave for 4 days to infuse.
4 Measure the liquid and add sugar, raisins, pearl barley, yeast spread on toast and the lemon and orange juice.
5 Leave in a warm place (65°F.–75°F.) to ferment.
6 When bubbling has ceased the wine should be stirred.
7 Leave for a further 3 days to settle.
8 Strain through flannel or *very thick* muslin into a cask, cork and leave for 6 months.
9 Pour into bottles, if not clear follow instructions on page 10 before bottling.
10 Cork and store in a *cool dark* place.

Parsnip wine (2)

Method and ingredients as for Parsnip wine (1), but use 3 lb. demerara sugar and about 6 cloves.

Sparkling parsnip wine

Use ingredients as for Parsnip wine (1) or (2) and follow the instructions, steps 1 to 5. Before bubbling has ceased, strain, bottle and cork, as Sparkling apple wine (see page 14).

Pea pod wine

you will need:

5 lb. peas and pods	1 gallon water

To each gallon juice:

3 lb. sugar	juice 1 lemon
½ oz. yeast	juice 1 orange

Method as for Potato wine (see below).

Potato wine (1)

you will need:

4 lb. potatoes	1½ oz. ginger
6 pints boiling water	

To each gallon juice:

2 lb. sugar	1 slice toast
4 oz. raisins	juice 1 lemon
8 oz. pearl barley	juice 1 orange
½ oz. yeast	

1 Wash and slice the potatoes, do not peel.
2 Pour the boiling water over them, adding the ginger.
3 Leave for 4 days to infuse.
4 Measure the liquid and add sugar, raisins, pearl barley, yeast spread on toast, and the lemon and orange juice.
5 Leave in warm place (65°F.–75°F.) to ferment.
6 When bubbling has ceased the wine should be stirred.
7 Leave for a further 3 days to settle.
8 Strain through flannel or *very thick* muslin into a cask, cork and leave for 6 months.
9 Pour into bottles, if not clear follow instructions on page 10 before bottling.
10 Cork and store in a *cool dark* place.

Potato wine (2)

you will need:

5 lb. potatoes	1 oz. ginger
1 gallon water	

To each gallon juice:

3 lb. demerara sugar	juice 2 lemons
½ oz. yeast	juice 1 orange

1 Put the potatoes into a pan.
2 Add the water and boil for 2–3 minutes.
3 Add the ginger and leave for 4 days to infuse.
4 Measure the liquid and add sugar, yeast and the fruit juices.
5 Leave in a warm place (65°F.–75°F.) to ferment.
6 When bubbling has ceased the wine should be stirred.
7 Leave for a further 3 days to settle.
8 Strain through flannel or *very thick* muslin into a cask, cork and leave for 6 months.
9 Pour into bottles, if not clear follow instructions on page 10 before bottling.
10 Cork and store in a *cool dark* place.

Potato and prune wine

you will need:

3 lb. potatoes	8 pints water
1 lb. dried prunes*	

To each gallon juice:

3 lb. brown sugar	½ oz. yeast
Juice 2 lemons	

* There is no need to soak the prunes.

1 Wash and slice the potatoes, but do not peel them.
2 Add to the prunes and pour over the boiling water.
3 Leave for 4 days to infuse. Strain.
4 Measure the liquid and add sugar, yeast and lemon juice.
5 Leave in a warm place (65°F.–75°F.) to ferment.
6 When bubbling has ceased the wine should be stirred.
7 Leave for a further 3 days to settle.
8 Strain through flannel or *very thick* muslin into a cask, cork and leave for 6 months.
9 Pour into bottles. If wine is not clear, follow instructions on page 10 before bottling.
10 Cork and store in a *cool dark* place.

Potato wine (3)

Method and ingredients as for Potato wine (2) but omit ginger and add 1 lb. raisins.

Potato wine (4)

Method as for Potato wine (1) but omit the ginger and the pearl barley and use 3 lb. potatoes and 1 lb. green grapes.

Sparkling potato wine

Use any of the recipes for potato wine, and follow the instructions, steps 1 to 5. Before fermentation ceases, strain, bottle and cork as Sparkling apple wine.

Sparkling potato and prune wine

Use ingredients as Potato and prune wine, and follow the method, steps 1 to 5. Just before fermenting comes to an end, strain, bottle and cork, as Sparkling apple wine.

Swede or turnip wine

you will need:

4 lb. swedes	6 pints water

To each gallon juice:

2–2½ lb. sugar	juice 1 orange
juice 2 lemons	½ oz. yeast

Method as for Potato wine (1) (see page 31).

Tomato wine

you will need:

8 lb. tomatoes	2 pints boiling water
pinch salt	

To each gallon juice:

2 lb. sugar	juice 2 lemons
½ oz. yeast	

1 Chop tomatoes and add sprinkling of salt.
2 Pour over the boiling water and press firmly.
3 Leave for 4 days to infuse. Strain.
4 Measure the liquid and add sugar, yeast and lemon juice.
5 Leave in a warm place (65°F.–75°F.) to ferment.
6 When bubbling has ceased the wine should be stirred.
7 Leave for a further 3 days to settle.
8 Strain through flannel or *very thick* muslin into a cask, cork and leave for 6 months.
9 Pour into bottles, if not clear follow instructions on page 10 before bottling.
10 Cork and store in a *cool dark* place.

Turnip wine

you will need:

4 lb. turnips	6 pints water

To each gallon juice:

2½–3 lb. sugar*	½ oz. yeast
juice 2 lemons	

*2½ lb. sugar will give a semi-sweet wine—3 lb. sugar will give a very sweet dessert wine.

1 Wash and slice the turnips.
2 Pour the boiling water over them and leave for 4 days to infuse.
3 Measure the liquid and add sugar, lemon juice and yeast.
4 Leave in a warm place (65°F.–75°F.) to ferment.
5 When bubbling has ceased the wine should be stirred.
6 Leave for a further 3 days to settle.
7 Strain through flannel or *very thick* muslin into a cask, cork and leave for 6 months.
8 Pour into bottles, if not clear follow instructions on page 10 before bottling.
9 Cork and store in a *cool dark* place.

Sparkling turnip wine

Use ingredients as Turnip wine and follow method, steps 1 to 4. Before bubbling ceases, strain, bottle and cork, as Sparkling apple wine.

Herb wine

Sage wine

You do not actually make wine from sage. You add a little crushed or finely chopped sage to a good red wine.
Let it stand in the bottle or jar for several days, shaking well.
Serve as ordinary red wine.
It was believed that this was a very excellent cure for aches and pains.

Parsley wine

you will need:

8 oz. parsley	3 lb. sugar
8 pints boiling water	juice of 1 lemon
1 oz. ginger	¼ oz. yeast

1 Simmer parsley and water for 10 minutes, then add the ginger.
2 Add sugar and lemon juice while still warm, then add yeast.
3 Leave in a warm place to ferment and continue as Potato wine (1).

Flower Wines

Since it will take a long time to pick flowers you must be very selective about the blossom. Imperfect or dirty blossom must not be used. It should be just full out, but not overblown.

Wash well and leave to dry a while, but if you feel they are slightly damp, reduce the amount of water in the recipe accordingly.

In the case of certain flowers a pint measure has been given as this is more convenient than weighing. Pack flowers loosely and *do not* push them down.

Flavour of flower wines

Broom . . . . dry white wine
Clover . . . . dry white wine
Cowslip . . . . . very light white wine
Dandelion . . light, often sparkling wine
Elderflower . . . . . light dry white wine
Primrose . . . . dry white wine
Rose petal . . . dark red roses produce a
pale vin rosé

Broom flower wine

you will need:

5 lb. broom flowers	3 lemons
3 oranges	1 gallon boiling water

To each gallon juice:

3 lb. sugar	½ oz. yeast

1 Put the broom flowers into a container.
2 Add the fruit rinds to the boiling water and pour over the flowers.
3 Allow to stand for 4 days, stirring from time to time.
4 Strain through flannel or several thicknesses of fine muslin.
5 Measure and stir in sugar, the juice from the fruit and yeast.
6 Keep in a warm room (65°F.–75°F.) and allow to ferment.
7 When you are sure all bubbling has ceased, stir the wine.
8 Allow 3 days to settle and strain again most carefully.
9 Put into a corked container (not bottles).
10 After several months maturing pour into bottles.

Clover wine

you will need:

6 pints purple clover flowers	8 pints boiling water

To each gallon juice:

juice 3 lemons	½ oz. yeast
juice 2 oranges	3 lb. sugar

Method as for Cowslip wine (see below).

Cowslip flower wine

you will need:

6 pints cowslip flowers	8 pints boiling water

To each gallon juice:

juice 3 lemons	½ oz. yeast
juice 2 oranges	3 lb. sugar

1 Cover the flowers with the boiling water.
2 Allow to stand for 4 days, stirring from time to time.
3 Strain through flannel or several thicknesses of fine muslin.
4 Measure and stir in the fruit juice, yeast and sugar.
5 Keep in a warm room (65°F.–75°F.) and allow to ferment.
6 When you are sure all bubbling has ceased, stir the wine.
7 Allow 3 days to settle.
8 Strain again most carefully.
9 Put into a corked container (not bottles).
10 After several months maturing pour into bottles.

Dandelion flower wine (1)

you will need:

1 oz. whole ginger	8 pints boiling water
5 pints dandelion flowers	

To each gallon juice:

3 lb. sugar	juice 1 orange
juice 1 lemon	½ oz. yeast

1 Put the ginger with the dandelion flowers.
2 Pour over the boiling water and allow to stand for 4 days, stirring from time to time.

3 Strain through flannel or several thicknesses of fine muslin.

4 Measure and stir in sugar, fruit juices and yeast.

5 Keep in a warm room (65°F.–75°F.) and allow to ferment.

6 When you are sure all bubbling has ceased, stir the wine.

7 Allow 3 days to settle.

8 Strain again most carefully.

9 Pour into a corked container (not bottles).

10 After several months maturing pour into bottles.

Dandelion flower wine (2)

you will need:

8 oz. raisins	8 pints boiling water
5 pints dandelion flowers	

To each gallon juice:

4 lb. brown sugar	juice 1 orange
juice 1 lemon	½ oz. yeast

1 Put the raisins with the dandelion flowers and continue as recipe (1).

Dry dandelion flower wine

Use either recipe for Dandelion flower wine, but in recipe (1) use 2¼ lb. sugar only and in recipe (2) use 2½ lb. sugar only.

Sparkling dandelion wine

Either of the above recipes are suitable for a sparkling dandelion wine. Follow method steps 1 to 5 and bottle before fermenting has ceased (see page 12).

Elderflower wine (1)

you will need:

1 oz. whole ginger or grated rind of 1 lemon	1 pint elderflowers
	8 pints boiling water

To each gallon juice:

3 lb. sugar	½ oz. yeast
juice 1 orange or 1 lemon	

1 Put the ginger or lemon rind with the elderflowers.

2 Pour over the boiling water.

3 Allow to stand for 4 days, stirring from time to time.

4 Strain through flannel or several thicknesses of fine muslin.

5 Measure and stir in the sugar, the orange or lemon juice and yeast.

6 Keep in a warm room (65°F.–75°F.) to ferment.

7 When you are sure all bubbling has ceased, stir the wine.

8 Allow 3 days to settle.

9 Strain again most carefully.

10 Put into a corked container (not bottles).

11 After several months maturing pour into bottles.

Elderflower wine (2)

you will need:

8 oz. raisins	1 pint elderflowers
6 cloves	8 pints boiling water

To each gallon juice:

3½ lb. demerara sugar (brown sugar)	juice 1 orange
juice 1 lemon	½ oz. yeast

1 Put the raisins and cloves with the elderflowers.

2 Continue as recipe (1).

Dry elderflower wine

On the whole most people prefer a sweet elderflower wine, but either of the above recipes are suitable for a dry wine but use 2½ lb. sugar in recipe (1) and 2¾ lb. in recipe (2).

Sparkling elderflower wine

Elderflowers are very suitable for sparkling wine.

Use either the sweet or dry recipes above, following steps 1 to 6 but bottle before fermentation ceases (see page 12).

Primrose wine

you will need:

6 pints primrose flowers	8 pints boiling water

To each gallon juice:

juice 3 lemons	½ oz. yeast
juice 2 oranges	3 lb. sugar

Method as for Cowslip wine (see page 34).

Rose petal wine

you will need:

4 pints rose petals*	8 pints water

To each gallon juice:

juice 2 lemons	3 lb. sugar
juice 1 orange	½ oz. yeast

* The choice of rose petals is rather important. Choose petals from fragrant roses and make sure they are not damaged by rain when using them. The roses should be just opened and freshly picked.

1 Cover the petals with the boiling water.
2 Allow to stand for 4 days, stirring from time to time.
3 Strain through flannel or several thicknesses of fine muslin.
4 Measure and stir in the fruit juice, sugar and yeast.
5 Keep in a warm room (65°F.–75°F.) and allow to ferment.
6 When you are sure bubbling has ceased, stir the wine.
7 Allow 3 days to settle.
8 Strain again most carefully.
9 Put into a corked container (not bottles).
10 After several months maturing pour into bottles.

Cereal Wines

The amount of yeast used in cereal wines appears rather high, but of course you have to ferment a great deal of natural starch and very little natural sugar.

Flavour of cereal wine

Barley, maize, rice, rye and wheat all produce a wine like a light port – very strong.

Maize wine

Method as for either Wheat wine recipes (see page 37), using maize in place of wheat.

Barley wine

Make as either recipe for Wheat wine (see page 37), using pearl barley in place of wheat.

Rice wine

you will need:

3 lb. medium or long grain rice	1 gallon boiling water
2½ lb. sugar	2 oz. yeast
1 lb. raisins	

1 Put the rice, sugar and raisins into a large container.
2 Pour over the boiling water and allow to become lukewarm.
3 Stir in the yeast.
3 Leave in the pan for 3 weeks, stirring from time to time.
5 Strain into a cask.
6 Allow to ferment and when bubbling has ceased cork or cover tightly (see page 11).
7 Leave for at least 6 months and preferably 1 year before bottling.

Rye wine

Method as either Wheat wine recipes (see page 37) using rye in place of wheat.

Wheat wine (1)

you will need:

1 pint wheat	8 pints boiling water
3½ lb. sugar	2 oz. yeast
2 lb. raisins	

1 Put the wheat, sugar and raisins into a large container.
2 Pour over the boiling water and allow to become lukewarm.
3 Stir in the yeast.
4 Leave in the pan for 3 weeks, stirring from time to time.
5 Strain into a cask.
6 Allow to ferment and when bubbling has ceased cork or cover tightly (see page 11).
7 Leave for at least 6 months and preferably 1 year before bottling.

Variation

With sultanas: lighter wine is produced if sultanas are used instead of raisins.

Wheat wine (2)

you will need:

1 pint wheat	2 lemons
4 lb. demerara sugar	8 pints boiling water
2 lb. raisins	2 oz. yeast
2 oranges	

1 Put the wheat, sugar, raisins and sliced oranges and lemons into a large container.
2 Pour over the boiling water and continue as for Wheat wine (1).

Malt wine

you will need:

2 lb. malt extract	1 gallon boiling water
2 lb. sugar	1 oz. yeast

1 Be very careful when buying the malt to buy only malt extract and not cod liver oil and malt.
2 Put the malt into the container with the sugar and pour over the boiling water.
3 Allow to become lukewarm, then stir in the yeast.
4 Leave for 1 week.
5 Strain into a cask and allow to ferment.
6 When fermentation has ceased, bottle and store for at least 6 months before using.

Cider, Perry, Beer and Mead

Cider

If you grow apples, or can buy them cheaply, it is worthwhile making your own cider. Following are recipes for making various ciders and perry, which is the drink made with pears. You will find from your own experience which apples you prefer, for obviously each apple gives its own individual flavour to the drink, but for your first attempt do choose a sharp juicy apple, not a mealy type which produces a poor flavoured juice.

Dry cider (1)

you will need:
sour apples

1 Choose sour apples—a good cooking apple is ideal, but make sure it is mature.
2 Leave them in a warmish place for several weeks until they are just beginning to soften.
3 Chop up and pound until they are a pulp.
4 Strain through muslin, pressing very hard so that all the juice is extracted.
5 Keep this juice in the pan in a warm place.
6 Allow to bubble.
7 When bubbles rise to the surface of the liquid and the sediment drops to the bottom, put into a cask.
8 Cover tightly.
9 Leave for 6–7 months in a cool place.
10 Strain and bottle.

Cider (2)

This cider is not quite as dry as Cider (1)

you will need:

4 lb. apples	1 lb. sugar
1 gallon boiling water	½ oz. yeast
8 oz. raisins	

1 Slice the fruit.
2 Cover with the boiling water, and add the raisins and sugar.
3 Leave for 3 days, stirring well each day, and then add the yeast.
4 Leave to ferment and when fermentation has ceased, strain.
5 The cider is then ready to bottle.

Sweet cider

you will need:
sour apples

To each gallon juice:

2½ lb. sugar	1 oz. yeast

1 Choose the same type of apples as for dry cider, but instead of leaving them to mature, cut them up.
2 Put them in a pan.
3 Cover with water.
4 Leave for 2 weeks, stirring every day.
5 Strain carefully and warm the liquid. Add sugar and yeast.
6 Cover and leave in a warm place to ferment.
7 When fermentation is beginning pour into casks.
8 Seal the casks at the end of fermentation.
9 Bottle at the end of 6 months.

Sparkling cider

you will need:
sour apples

Follow exactly the same process as for dry cider (see above) but carefully watch the liquid in the cask and when fermenting well strain into bottles. The bottles should be corked and wired down.

Speedy cider

you will need:

3 lb. cooking apples	3 juicy lemons
6 quarts water	1 oz. bruised ginger
2 lb. granulated sugar	(optional)

1 Wipe the apples, cut into pieces and put through the mincer together with the peel and core.
2 Place in an earthenware bowl and pour on the fresh cold water.
3 Leave for 7 days, stirring well night and morning.
4 Strain the liquor carefully.
5 Mix it with the sugar, grated lemon rind and strained lemon juice.
6 Leave for 24 hours.
7 Strain and bottle in screw topped bottles.
8 Bruised ginger may be added if wished with the lemon.

The cider will be fit to drink in a week, but it improves if kept a few months.

Perry (pear cider)

For dry perry

you will need:
firm but juicy pears

Prepare in the same way as for dry cider (see above), using pears instead of apples.

For sweet perry

1 Chop the pears to a pulp.
2 Add water.
3 Proceed as for sweet cider.
4 Allow 2½ lb. raisins and 3 lb. sugar and 1 oz. yeast to each gallon of juice.

To make your own beer

If you make real beer at home you will need malted barley to give the real effect.

Ginger beer or pop

you will need:

To start beer:	To flavour:
½ oz. yeast	1½ lb. sugar
¾ pint warm water	2 pints water
2 teaspoons ginger	juice 2 lemons
2 teaspoons sugar	

To feed plant:	To dilute:
6 teaspoons ground ginger	5 pints water
6 teaspoons sugar	

1 Mix together ingredients for starting beer. Stir well, leave for 24 hours, then feed daily.
2 Feed with 1 teaspoon ground ginger and 1 teaspoon sugar each day.
3 After 7 days strain plant through cloth.
4 To flavour, dissolve the sugar with the water.
5 Add the lemon juice and liquid from the plant, i.e. the yeast mixture.
6 To dilute, add all this to the 5 pints of water.
7 Mix well.
8 Bottle in screw top bottles.
9 Keep for 7 days to mature, then use.

Note

As the ginger beer is not particularly alcoholic it is suitable for all the family.

Quick ginger beer

you will need:

1 lb. sugar	1 gallon boiling water
1 oz. cream of tartar	½ oz. yeast
1 oz. ground ginger	

1 Mix all the ingredients except the yeast together.
2 Allow to become lukewarm and stir in the yeast.
3 Strain and bottle.
4 Cork down tightly, tying the corks and leaving overnight. It will then be ready to serve.

Hop beer

you will need:

1 lb. sugar	1 gallon boiling water
½ oz. hops	1 oz. yeast
1 lb. malt extract	

1 Boil all the ingredients together except the yeast for 1 hour.
2 Strain and if less than a gallon of liquid, add a little more water.
3 Cool and add the yeast.
4 Leave in covered container for 3 days in a warm room (65°F.–75°F.).
5 Strain, or preferably syphon and bottle.
6 Tie corks down or wire them and leave for approximately 1 week to mature.

Variation

With ginger: You can add ½ oz. root ginger to flavour or use brown sugar in place of white.

Nettle beer (or nettle pop)

you will need:

2 lb. nettles	2 oz. hops
2 gallons water	4 oz. sarsaparilla
½ oz. bruised root ginger	1½ lb. castor sugar
4 lb. malt	1 oz. yeast

1 Young nettles only should be used for this.
2 Wash well and put into a pan with the water, ginger, malt, hops and sarsaparilla.
3 Boil for 15 minutes.
4 Strain it over the sugar and stir until sugar has dissolved.
5 Add creamed yeast and when the beer starts to ferment, put it into bottles.
6 Cork these and tie down with string.

This beer is now ready to drink.

Nettle beer (2)

you will need:

2 lb. nettles (without roots)	1 lb. sugar
2 lemons	1 oz. cream of tartar
1 gallon boiling water	1 oz. yeast

1 Put the nettles, lemon rind and boiling water into a pan and boil for 15 minutes.
2 Strain into a container and add lemon juice, sugar and cream of tartar.
3 Allow to cool, then add the yeast.
4 Leave in lightly covered container in a warm room (65°F.–75°F.) for 3 days.
5 Strain into bottles, cork down and wire and leave for 1 week.

Mead

This is one of the oldest of drinks and honey is the main ingredient.

You do need a good honey. Various mead experts will each extort the virtues of their particular type of honey for mead. A light coloured honey gives the most attractive colour to the drink.

Mead (1)

This is one of the traditional drinks and it has a lovely flavour. Be very patient about storing your mead. After fermentation has ceased, you could keep it in a cask for some months before bottling and then keep the bottles for several years if possible.

you will need:

1 gallon water	1 oz. yeast (mead
3 lb. honey	yeast if obtainable)

1 Boil the water and allow to cool to approximately 130°F.
2 Pour over the warmed honey and stir together.
3 Cool, then add yeast.
4 Leave in a warm room (65°F.–75°F.) to ferment.
5 When fermentation ceases, allow to stand in a cool place for 2 weeks.
6 Strain or preferably syphon into a clean jar or cask.
7 Store for 6 months, then strain into bottles, wiring on corks.

Mead (2)

you will need:

4 lb. light honey	rind and juice
8 pints water	2 lemons
1 oz. hops	1 oz. yeast
½ oz. root ginger	¼ oz. isinglass

1 Dissolve honey in water and add hops, ginger and sliced rind and juice of lemons.
2 Boil for 45 minutes.
3 Strain into cask up to the brim.
4 While still lukewarm add yeast.
5 Allow to ferment—this will take approximately 5 weeks.
6 When bubbling has ceased put in isinglass dissolved in a little water.
7 Bung tightly. Keep for 6 months.
8 Strain into bottles. Wire on corks.

Sweet mead

Use either of the Mead recipes, but increase the amount of sugar to 6 lb.

Heather flavoured honey is particularly good in a sweet mead.

Sparkling mead

1 Make either of the Mead recipes above.
2 Allow to ferment and store, as suggested, in the cask.
3 At the end of 6 months measure and to each gallon add a syrup of 2 oz. sugar or warmed honey and ¼ pint warm water.
4 Make sure the honey or sugar is dissolved, then put into strong bottles and cork and wire down.

If wished a very little lemon juice could be added to the sugar or honey and water syrup.

Liqueurs and Spirits

To make your own liqueurs sounds a very difficult process. In actual fact, as you will see, it could not be easier.

You infuse the fruit with brandy, whisky, etc., as given in the recipes. Choose very sound and preferably ripe fruit so that you extract the maximum of mature juice.

You can also make the less usual home-made liqueurs, such as advocaat, shrubs, and strained fruit infusions of gin and rum, which will enable you to give a wonderful selection of drinks.

Advocaat

you will need:

6 large egg yolks	¾–1 bottle brandy
1 oz. castor sugar (little less if wished)	

1 Put the egg yolks and sugar into a bowl.
2 Stand this over a pan of hot water.
3 Beat until a smooth thick creamy consistency.
4 Beat until cool.
5 Gradually add the brandy, stirring continuously.
6 Bottle.

Apricot brandy

you will need:

ripe apricots	To each 1 lb. apricots:
brandy	4 oz. sugar

1 Halve the apricots, crack the stones and take out the kernels.
2 Put into bottles, allowing enough to half fill each bottle.
3 Add the sugar and fill the bottle with brandy.
4 Cover tightly and leave for 3–4 months, shaking occasionally.
5 Strain into another bottle.

Blackberry brandy

you will need:

blackberries	brandy
To each 1 lb. blackberries:	
2 cloves	3 oz. sugar or crushed
small pieces cinnamon	sugar candy

1 Slightly crush the blackberries.
2 Put enough into bottles to half fill each bottle.
3 Add cloves, cinnamon and sugar and fill the bottle with brandy.
4 Cover tightly and leave for 3–4 months, shaking occasionally.
5 Strain into another bottle.

Blackcurrant brandy

you will need:

blackcurrants	brandy
To each 1 lb. blackcurrants:	
1 small piece cinnamon	6 oz. sugar

Method as Blackberry brandy above.

Cherry brandy

you will need:

cherries*	brandy
To each 1 lb. cherries:	
1–2 cloves	2–3 oz. castor sugar

* morello cherries are best

1 Prick the cherries with a wooden cocktail stick.
2 Half fill a bottle with cherries.
3 Add cloves and sugar.
4 Fill the bottle with brandy.
5 Cover tightly.
6 Leave for 3–4 months, shaking bottles occasionally.
7 Strain into another bottle.

Greengage brandy

you will need:

ripe greengages	To each 1 lb.
brandy	greengages:
	4 oz. sugar

Method as Apricot brandy.

Orange brandy

you will need:

3 oranges*	brandy
4 oz. sugar	

* When Seville oranges are in season these produce the finest result.

1 Pare off the peel of the oranges and put into bottles with the sugar—do not use the juice.
2 Cover with brandy.
3 Cover tightly and leave for 3–4 months, shaking occasionally.
4 Strain into another bottle.

Peach brandy

you will need:

ripe peaches   brandy

To each 1 lb. peaches:
4 oz. sugar (preferably demerara sugar)

Method as Apricot brandy (see page 41).

Pineapple brandy

you will need:

fresh pineapple	brandy

To each 1 lb. pineapple:

2 cloves	6–8 oz. sugar

1 Peel and dice the pineapple.
2 Half fill a bottle with the fruit and add cloves and sugar.
3 Fill the bottles with brandy and cover tightly.
4 Leave for 3–4 months, shaking bottles occasionally.
5 Strain into another bottle.

Strawberry brandy

you will need:

strawberries   brandy

To each 1 lb. strawberries:

4 oz. sugar	finely pared rind 1 lemon

1 Crush the strawberries slightly.
2 Half fill bottles with strawberries, adding sugar and lemon rind.
3 Fill the bottles with brandy and cover tightly.
4 Leave for 3–4 months, shaking bottles occasionally.
5 Strain into another bottle.

Damson port

you will need:

8 pints water	4 lb. sugar
4 lb. damsons	½ pint boiling water

1 Pour the boiling water over the damsons.
2 Leave until next day.
3 Mash and stir daily for 5 days.
4 Strain through a jelly bag.
5 Add the sugar and ½ pint boiling water.
6 Leave to ferment for 8 days.
7 Skim, strain and bottle.

Fruit gins

Use exactly the same recipes as for fruit brandies, but use half the amount of sugar and top with gin.

The exception is Sloe gin where a high percentage of sugar is used, due to the 'bite' of the fruit.

Sloe gin

you will need:

sloes   gin*

To each 1 lb. sloes:
6 oz. sugar

*If using unsweetened gin double the amount of sugar.

1 Prick the ripe sound sloes all over with a needle.
2 Half fill glass jars with them.
3 Sprinkle with granulated sugar, cover with gin.
4 Keep tightly corked in a fairly warm place for 3 months, shaking the jars occasionally.
5 Strain through flannel or filter into bottles.
6 Cork tightly.

This gin greatly improves with keeping.

Blackberry whisky

you will need:

blackberries   whisky

To each 1 lb. blackberries:

2 cloves	1½ oz. sugar
1 small piece cinnamon	

1 Slightly crush the blackberries.
2 Half fill each bottle with the fruit.
3 Add cloves, cinnamon and sugar and fill the bottle with whisky.
4 Cover tightly and leave for 3–4 months.
5 Strain into another bottle.

Cherry whisky

you will need:

cherries	whisky

To each 1 lb. cherries:

1–2 cloves	1–1½ oz. castor sugar

1 Prick the cherries with a wooden cocktail stick.
2 Half fill a bottle with the fruit.
3 Add cloves and sugar and fill the bottle with whisky.
4 Cover tightly and leave for 3–4 months, shaking occasionally.
5 Strain into another bottle.

Rice 'whisky'

you will need:

3 lb. Carolina or short grain rice	juice 1 lemon
1 lb. raisins	8 pints warm water
3 lb. sugar	1 oz. yeast

1 Put the rice and chopped raisins with the sugar, lemon juice and water into a large bowl.
2 Add the yeast which should have been dissolved in a little warm water.
3 Let mixture stand, covered with a cloth, for 12 days, but stir occasionally for first 3 days.
4 See that it is kept in a warm place.
5 A scum will rise to the top as it works, but do not remove until the last day.
6 Filter the wine into a clean cask or a stone jar.

7 Store for 6 months in a cool place.
8 Bottle.

This is similar in taste, colour and potency to whisky.

Marrow rum

you will need:

3 lb. diced marrow	2 lemons

To each pint juice:

6 oz. castor sugar	1½ pints rum

1 Simmer marrow with lemon juice and pared rind until pulp.
2 Put through jelly bag.
3 Add the sugar and the rum.
4 Stir until sugar has dissolved.
5 Filter and bottle.

Alternative method

1 Make a hole in the centre of the marrow.
2 Into this put brown sugar and rum.
3 Suspend the marrow with a bowl underneath to catch the drips and the marrow-flavoured rum will drip through.

Shrubs

Shrubs are made in exactly the same way as the fruit brandies but you use a rather higher percentage of sugar to give a very thick rich infusion.

Tea and Coffee

Tea

As well as iced tea, there are several old country recipes for herb teas in this section. These may seem a little strange, but they were considered in the past extremely good for cleansing the blood and many people still find they are a very palatable drink.

To make good tea

A good cup of tea, as most people will agree, is one of the most satisfying beverages of all. There are, however, certain rules that make a great deal of difference to the perfection of the tea.

1 You should use freshly drawn water.
2 If there is water already in the kettle, throw it away and take the water from the cold mains supply.
3 Let the water come to the boil, but do not let it go on boiling for any length of time.
4 When the water is nearly boiling pour some into your tea-pot to make sure this is thoroughly heated. Pour it away as the kettle boils and put in the tea.
5 Your choice of tea is entirely a matter of personal taste and it is an interesting point that however good a tea may be, one is inclined to tire of it and a change of brand is advisable.
6 The old ruling 1 teaspoon per person and 1 for the pot is fairly sound for small families, but in a large family you may find you need slightly less than this.
7 Take the tea-pot to the kettle and pour the water on to the tea, while it is still boiling.
8 Stir briskly, put the lid on the tea-pot and let it infuse for several minutes. You will then have a perfect pot of tea.
9 To give a really perfect cup of tea, choose your cups with care. Some people will only enjoy tea from a very thin cup. Remember that rather wide cups will allow the tea to cool down very quickly.
10 Real connoisseurs of tea like to warm the cups with hot water and there is always discussion as to whether it is better to put in the milk before the tea or after. This you must try and find out for yourself.
11 If serving china tea, it is usual to have no milk and slices of lemon.

Tea for wine cups, etc.

If making tea for wine cups, do not make it too strong. Your tea should be only a pale amber colour and china tea is often a very good choice.

Blackcurrant tea

you will need for 1 glass:

1 good teaspoon blackcurrant jam (little more if wished)	very hot or boiling water squeeze lemon juice (optional)

1 Put the jam into the bottom of a warm glass.
2 Fill up with the water, adding lemon juice if used.

Dandelion tea

you will need:

To each 2 pints boiling water:

about ¼ pint dandelion leaves

1 Pour boiling water over the chopped washed dandelion leaves.
2 Leave to infuse for a short time.
3 Strain.

Herb tea

The most usual herbs to use are sage, lemon thyme, a little camomile or you can take a mixture of these. They are supposed to be extremely soothing when people have a temperature.

you will need:

2 pints boiling water	2 oz. sugar
1 oz. freshly chopped herbs	juice 1–2 lemons

1 Pour the boiling water over the herbs.
2 Stir and leave to infuse for a while.
3 If intending to serve cold, add the sugar and lemon juice at once.
4 Strain over ice if possible.
5 If serving hot pour out as if serving a cup of tea and serve with a little sugar and slices of lemon separately.

Iced tea

you will need for 3–4 glasses:

1 pint hot tea	½ lemon
sugar to taste	mint leaves
crushed ice	sliced lemon

1 Make the tea, adding sugar to taste.
2 Pour over crushed ice in a bowl.
3 Add the lemon juice and pour into tall glasses.
4 Serve with a slice of lemon and a mint leaf floating in each glass.

Variation

With orange: add the juice of ½ orange instead of lemon.

Mint tea

As Herb tea, but use fresh mint and if possible one of the rather specialist mints—lemon mint or pineapple mint.

Raspberry leaf tea

you will need:

2 pints boiling water	2 oz. sugar
1 oz. chopped raspberry leaves	juice 1–2 lemons

1 Pour the boiling water over the leaves.
2 Infuse as ordinary tea.
3 Serve with sugar and lemon juice to taste.

Russian tea

you will need:

tea	little rum
lemon slices	

1 Make your tea in the usual way.
2 Pour into cups.
3 Add a little rum and top with slices of lemon.

To make good coffee

1 Coffee loses its flavour quickly, so do not buy too much at a time, and store in airtight tins or screw-topped jars.
2 Use the right amount of coffee—most people will like coffee made from 4 dessertspoons to 1 pint water—although this may be a little too strong if drinking black coffee.
3 Medium ground coffee is ideal for a percolator, jug method or saucepan method. A coarse coffee is quite good for a filter although it does tend to be a little wasteful.
4 Never use boiled milk with coffee. Cold or warm milk preserves the best flavour.

Jug method

Put coffee into a warm jug, pour over boiling water, stir briskly, leave to infuse for several minutes. Ideally this should be strained into another jug.

Saucepan method

Bring the water to the boil, add the coffee, stir briskly. Leave in a warm place to infuse several minutes. Strain.
OR heat coffee and water together but do not boil for any length of time.

Percolator method

Pack coffee into basket. Bring water to the boil. Leave to infuse for several minutes. If not using a thermostat, do not allow to percolate for too long a period.

Filter method

Put the coffee into the filter part, gradually pour over boiling water, allowing the coffee to drip through.

Vacuum top

Put coffee into top container, cold water into base. Allow to boil and infuse for several minutes in the top container, turning the heat low to stop splashing; there will always be a small quantity of water left in the bottom container. Remove from heat and allow to run back into the base. You can do this twice if wished.

Instant coffee

Put a little soluble coffee powder into warm cups or jug. Pour over hot or boiling water. Stir briskly.

Coffee cream soda

you will need for 4 glasses:

1¼–1½ pints strong coffee	sugar to taste
4 tablespoons vanilla or coffee ice cream	1 jar or can or ¼ pint thick cream

1 Make the coffee and allow to get really cold.
2 Put 1 tablespoon of ice cream in the bottom of each glass. Use tall glasses.
3 Fill to within an inch of the top with the coffee.
4 Add a little sugar if wished.
5 Whip the cream and pile or pipe on top just before serving.

Frosted iced coffee

you will need for 1 glass:

frosting (see page 7)	sugar to taste
little cracked ice	1 tablespoon coffee or
¾ tumbler ice cold coffee	vanilla ice cream

1 First frost the rim of the glass.
2 Put the ice in the tumbler, add the ice cold coffee.
3 Sweeten to taste.
4 Top with ice cream.

Iced coffee

1 Make coffee in your favourite way and allow to get very cold in the refrigerator.
2 Pour over crushed ice and top with mint or slices of lemon.
3 If preferred, pour over ice cream or over crushed ice and top with a little lightly whipped cream.

Irish coffee

This has become very popular in the last few years and besides not being very difficult to make gives a new flavour to after-dinner coffee. Serve in glasses rather than cups, although it can be served in an ordinary warmed cup.

you will need:

Irish whiskey	thick cream
strong black coffee	sugar

1 Put the whiskey into the glasses, the amount depending on personal taste.
2 Add the coffee and the sugar.
3 Stir vigorously.
4 Very slowly pour the cream over the back of a spoon into the coffee. It should form a thick layer of cream resting on the coffee.
5 Sip the coffee mixture through the layer of cream.

Granita di caffé soda

you will need for 8–10 glasses:

1 pint very strong black coffee	whipped cream approximately 1 pint
sugar to taste	soda water

1 Make very strong coffee adding sugar to taste.
2 Allow to cool and pour in the ice trays of a refrigerator.
3 When beginning to set round the sides of the trays, stir with a knife.
4 Freeze for approximately 2 hours until the mixture has a crumbly consistency, stirring with a knife at approximately 30 minute intervals throughout.
5 Pour into glasses and top with lightly whipped cream, half filling the glasses only.
6 Fill up with soda water.

Mocha coffee

you will need for 3–4 glasses:

¼ pint very strong cold coffee	1 pint coffee ice cream
5 tablespoons melted chocolate	*To decorate:* little grated chocolate

1 Put all the ingredients into a bowl and beat to a smooth consistency.
2 Pour into glasses and sprinkle with chocolate.

Spiced coffee

you will need for 4 glasses:

1¼–1½ pints strong coffee	sugar
1 teaspoon mixed spice	1 jar or can or ¼ pint thick cream
ice cubes	little grated nutmeg

1 Make the coffee and add the mixed spice.
2 Allow to get really cold.
3 Put ice cubes at the bottom of 4 tall glasses.
4 Fill to within an inch of the top with the coffee.
4 Add a little sugar if wished.
6 Whip the cream and pile or pipe on top just before serving.
7 Sprinkle nutmeg over the cream.

Turkish coffee

This is a very strong, very sweet brew of coffee and should only be served to those who have acquired a taste for it. To make the coffee you use a very fine blend of pulverised coffee which can be bought from good coffee merchants. For most people you use 4 heaped tablespoons to a ¼ pint of water.

1 Make the coffee by pouring the boiling water on to the coffee in a pan.
2 Bring to the boil.
3 Remove from heat.
4 Repeat this twice so that each time it froths up.
5 Add 3 or 4 times the usual amount of sugar for each cup.
6 A few drops of cold water added to the coffee makes any grounds sink to the bottom.

Instant powdered coffee can be used and you need approximately 8 times your normal quantity.

Viennese iced coffee

you will need for 4 glasses:

1¼–1½ pints strong coffee	1 jar or can or ¼ pint thick cream
ice cubes	little grated chocolate
sugar to taste	

1 Make the coffee and allow to get really cold.
2 Put ice cubes at the bottom of 4 tall glasses.
3 Fill to within an inch of the top with the coffee.
4 Add a little sugar if wished.
5 Whip the cream and pile or pipe on top just before serving.
6 Sprinkle chocolate over the cream.

Soft Drinks

There are a number of very good prepared squashes on the market, but nothing is more delicious or thirst quenching than a home-made fruit drink.
These drinks can, of course, be served hot or cold.

Appleade

you will need for 2–3 glasses:

about 1 lb. apples	sugar or glucose to taste
rind and juice 1 lemon	
1 pint boiling water	

1 Wash the apples and cut them into pieces, retaining peel and core.
2 Add the pieces of lemon rind.
3 Pour over the boiling water, then leave until cold.
4 Strain and add sugar or glucose and lemon juice.

Gooseberryade

you will need for 8 glasses:
1 lb. ripe gooseberries   1½ pints water
2 sliced lemons   ¼ pint soda water
sugar to taste

To decorate:
lemon slices

1 Put the gooseberries and sliced lemons into a saucepan with the sugar.
2 Add the water and bring to the boil.
3 Simmer for a few minutes until gooseberries are tender.
4 Take off the heat and allow to cool.
5 Pour off the juice and dilute with the soda water.
6 Serve in glasses, adding gooseberries and lemon slices to decorate.

Grapefruit drink

you will need for 2–3 glasses:
1 pint boiling water   sugar or glucose to
1 large grapefruit   taste

1 Grate about 1 teaspoon of rind from the grapefruit.
2 Pour into a jug and pour over the freshly boiling water.
3 Add the grapefruit juice and sugar or glucose.
4 Leave until cold and strain.

Lemonade

you will need for 2–3 glasses:
2 small lemons   sugar or glucose to
1 pint boiling water   taste

1 Grate the rind from the lemons, being careful to use only the yellow zest.
2 Put into a jug, pour over the freshly boiling water.
3 Add the lemon juice, sugar or glucose.
4 Leave until cold and strain.

Old fashioned lemonade

you will need for 6–8 glasses:
3 lemons   ice, if available
3 tablespoons sugar   1 or 2 extra slices
2 pints water   lemon
1 sprig mint

1 Wipe unpeeled lemons and cut into dice, being careful not to lose any juice.
2 Put into a jug with the sugar.
3 Pour on the boiling water and leave for 15–30 minutes until strong without becoming bitter.
4 Strain.
5 Put the mint into the serving jug with ice if available and slices of fresh lemon an hour before the lemonade is required.

Lemon mintade

Use either of the recipes for lemonade above, but add a few crushed mint leaves. Strain, and serve topped with a sprig of mint.

Orangeade

(Illustrated on the cover)

you will need for 2–3 glasses:
2 oranges   sugar to taste
1 pint boiling water

1 Grate the rind from the oranges, being careful to use only the orange zest.
2 Put into a jug, pour over the freshly boiling water.
3 Add the orange juice and sugar.
4 Leave until cold and strain.

Pineappleade

(illustrated on the cover)

you will need for 4–6 glasses:
1 large can pineapple   1½ pints water
  chunks   2–3 oz. sugar
rind and juice 3   soda water
  lemons

1 Chop the pineapple finely, being careful the juice is not wasted.
2 Put the pineapple, lemon rind and juice, pineapple syrup, water and sugar into a pan.
3 Bring to the boil and simmer gently for 1–2 minutes.
4 Allow to cool.
5 Dilute with soda water when serving.
6 Serve with crushed ice.

Raspberryade

you will need for 6 glasses:

1 lb. ripe raspberries	sugar to taste
2 lemons	½ pint soda water
1½ pints boiling water	

Method as Strawberryade (see below).

Rhubarbade

(*Illustrated on the cover*)

you will need for 6 glasses:

1 lb. ripe rhubarb, cut in 1-inch pieces	3 oz. sugar
	1½ pints water
2 sliced lemons	½ pint soda water

1 Put the rhubarb and sliced lemons into a saucepan with the sugar.
2 Add the water.
3 Bring to the boil and simmer for a few minutes until the rhubarb is tender.
4 Take off the heat and allow to cool.
5 Pour off juice and dilute with soda water.
6 Serve in glasses, adding the rhubarb and lemon slices to decorate.

Strawberryade

you will need for 6 glasses:

1 lb. ripe strawberries	sugar to taste
2 sliced lemons	½ pint soda water
1½ pints boiling water	

1 Put the strawberries and sliced lemons into a tall jug.
2 Pour over the boiling water, adding sugar to taste.
3 Allow to cool.
4 Pour off juice and dilute with soda water.
5 Serve in glasses, adding strawberries and lemon slices to decorate.

Blackberry cordial

you will need:

1 pint white vinegar	1 lb. loaf sugar
2 lb. ripe blackberries	8 oz. honey

1 Pour the vinegar over the blackberries.
2 Allow to stand in an earthenware jar for 7–8 days, stirring occasionally to extract the juices.
3 Strain off when ready and put the liquor in an enamel saucepan with the sugar and honey.
4 Bring to the boil.

5 Remove from the heat and allow to get cold.
6 Bottle and cork and keep in a dark place.
7 Excellent diluted with hot water for sore throats.

Citrus fruit cordial

It is possible to make a rather concentrated citrus fruit drink. While this does not keep indefinitely, it is sufficiently strong to dilute with water or soda water as wished and it is, therefore, very practical if you are short of storage space.

you will need:

1 grapefruit	2 lemons
3 oranges	½ pint water

To each ½ pint liquid:
3–4 oz. sugar

1 Pare off the rinds (which should be paper thin) of the fruit.
2 Put into a saucepan with the water and simmer gently in covered pan for 5 minutes—no more.
3 Strain and add the juice of the fruits.
4 Measure and add sugar.
5 Heat to dissolve the sugar and store in jugs.

Honey and lemon drink

you will need for 4 glasses:

2 tablespoons honey*	¾ pint boiling water
2 tablespoons lemon juice*	

* Both the honey and lemon can be increased if wished.

1 Blend the honey and lemon together.
2 Pour over the boiling water.

Lemon cordial

you will need:

6 lemons	*To each ½ pint liquid:*
½ pint boiling water	3–4 oz. sugar

1 Pare off the rind (which should be paper thin) from the lemons.
2 Put into a saucepan with the water and simmer gently in a covered pan for 6 minutes only.
3 Strain and add the juice of the lemons.
4 Measure the liquid and add the sugar.
5 Heat to dissolve the sugar and store in jugs.

Orange cordial

you will need:

6 oranges
1 lemon
½ pint water

To each ½ pint liquid:
3–4 oz. sugar

1 Pare off the rinds (which should be paper thin) of the lemon and oranges.
2 Put into a saucepan with the water and simmer gently in covered pan for 5 minutes only.
3 Strain and add the juice of the fruits.
4 Measure and add the sugar.
5 Heat to dissolve the sugar and store in jugs.

Boston cream drink

you will need for 4 tumblers:

2 pints boiling water
½ oz. cream of tartar
juice 1 large lemon
1 egg white
   (unbeaten)

2 tablespoons sugar,
   glucose or honey
pinch bicarbonate of
   soda

To decorate:
lemon slices

1 Put all ingredients, except the bicarbonate of soda, into a jug.
2 Strain into glasses.
3 Add the bicarbonate of soda. This causes the drink to fizz so do not fill the glasses too full.
4 Decorate with slices of lemon.

Winter cordial

you will need for 4–6 glasses:

4 dessertspoons
   oatmeal
2 dessertspoons
   demerara sugar

½ teaspoon ground
   ginger
1 lemon
2 pints boiling water

1 Mix oatmeal, sugar and ground ginger together in a basin.
2 Grate the rind of the lemon and add to the oatmeal mixture.
3 Gradually pour in the boiling water, stirring all the time.
4 Put into a saucepan, add lemon juice and simmer for 10 minutes.
5 Strain and serve hot.

This drink is excellent on cold nights.

An ancient barley drink

you will need:

2 oz. pearl barley
5 pints boiling water
2 oz. stoned raisins

2 oz. sliced figs
½ oz. liquorice root

1 Wash and blanch the pearl barley.
2 Add 4 pints of the water and cook until reduced to half.
3 Strain and add the raisins, figs and remaining water to the barley water.
4 Simmer again until reduced to 2 pints, adding the liquorice root just before cooking is completed.
5 Strain and serve diluted or undiluted.

This drink can be served hot or cold.

Bramble and lemon

you will need for 1 glass:

1 tablespoon bramble
   jelly
2 tablespoons water

juice 1 lemon
cold water or soda
   water

1 Heat the bramble jelly and water until the jelly is well dissolved.
2 Add the lemon juice.
3 Pour into a glass and top with soda water or water.

Hot lemon ginger

you will need:

rind and juice 2
   lemons
4 oz. root ginger

2 pints water
8 oz. sugar

1 Put the lemon rind, ginger and water into a pan.
2 Boil together until the mixture has been reduced to half.
3 Add the sugar and lemon juice.
4 Boil again until fairly thick and syrupy.
5 Strain into bottles and dilute with hot water as required.

If keeping for any length of time, it is better to put into bottling jars. This drink is considered very soothing for colds, etc.

Iced blackcurrant juice

you will need for 4 glasses:

5 tablespoons blackcurrant juice	$\frac{1}{2}$ teaspoon ground cloves
1 pint water	ice

1 Mix the blackcurrant juice, water and ground cloves.
2 Place in a jug.
3 Add the ice and allow to become really cold.

Iced lemon ginger

you will need for 1 glass:

1 small cube ice	1 teaspoon sugar
juice $\frac{1}{2}$ lemon	ginger ale

1 Put the ice in the bottom of a glass.
2 Add the lemon juice, sugar and fill up with ginger ale.

Lemon soda

you will need for 1 glass:

2 tablespoons fresh lemon juice	2 teaspoons sugar
	soda water

1 Put the lemon juice and sugar into a glass.
2 Fill up with soda water.

Orange soda

Use 2 tablespoons orange juice in place of lemon.

Grapefruit soda

Use grapefruit juice instead of lemon juice.

Lemon ice cream soda

you will need for 1 glass:

2 tablespoons fresh lemon juice	soda water
2 teaspoons sugar	1 tablespoon ice cream

1 Put the lemon juice and sugar into a glass.
2 Fill two-thirds of the glass with the soda water.
3 Top with ice cream and serve with a straw and spoon.

Orange ice cream soda

Use orange juice in place of lemon.

Grapefruit ice cream soda

Use grapefruit juice instead of lemon juice.

Pineapple serenade

you will need for 8–10 glasses:

2 oz. castor sugar	4 tablespoons sugar syrup (see page 54)
1 pint boiling water	
1 large can pineapple pieces	
2 pints canned pineapple juice	

To garnish:

pineapple	
ice	mint leaves

1 Dissolve sugar in boiling water.
2 Drain pineapple pieces and add juice to boiling water.
3 Mix well with pineapple juice and sugar syrup. Chill.
4 Serve in tall glasses, garnished with several pieces of pineapple, ice and mint leaves.

Redcurrant and lemon

you will need for 1 glass:

1 tablespoon redcurrant jelly	juice 1 lemon
2 tablespoons water	cold water or soda water

1 Heat the redcurrant jelly and water until the jelly is well dissolved.
2 Add the lemon juice.
3 Pour into a glass and top with soda water or water.

Note

This also makes a very pleasant hot drink.

Summertime soda

(Illustrated on the cover)

you will need for 1 glass:

juice 1 orange	soda water
juice 1 lemon	ice cream
juice 1 grapefruit	

1 Put all the fruit juices in a long tumbler.
2 Fill almost to the top with soda water.
3 Add a spoonful of ice cream.
4 Serve immediately.

Fruit fluffs

1 Follow the directions for lemonade, orangeade, etc., on page 48 or use diluted cordials or squashes.
2 Two-thirds fill cold glasses with the mixture, then add the stiffly beaten white of an egg, dividing this between two glasses.
3 The egg white floats on the top and looks very attractive.

If you would rather blend the egg white with the drink put in a basin with the liquid and then pour carefully into glasses.

Gooseberry fluff

you will need for 2 glasses:

1 lb. gooseberries	*To decorate:*
2 sliced lemons	few sprigs mint
3 oz. sugar	
¾ pint water	
1½ pints soda water	

1 Put most of the gooseberries and sliced lemons into a saucepan with the sugar.
2 Add the water.
3 Bring to the boil and simmer for 2 minutes until the gooseberries just split.
4 Take off the heat and allow to cool.
5 Put a little of the liquid into the bottom of tumblers.
6 Top with soda water just before serving.
7 Decorate with gooseberries, lemon slices and mint.

Fruit Syrups

All fruit syrups can be kept well—they tend to have a better flavour and a thicker consistency if sugar is added—but they can be preserved without if it should be necessary for medical reasons.

1 Put the fruit into the top of a double saucepan or basin over hot water, adding the water if required. Press down the fruit to squash it well and cook for about 1 hour until you are sure all the juice is extracted. Press down during cooking.
2 Strain through a jelly bag, or through several thicknesses of muslin over a fine sieve.
3 Measure the juice and add sugar, allowing approximately 8 oz. sugar to 1 pint juice, heat together until the sugar is dissolved, stirring well during this time. *Do not continue boiling* when sugar has dissolved.
4 Pour the hot syrup into hot bottling jars or use cordial bottles with well fitting screw top lids, which should have been boiled before using.
5 Allow syrup to cool in the bottles, which should not be quite filled.

6 Stand them in a steriliser or deep pan with a rack at the bottom, or several thicknesses of cloth or paper.
7 Loosen screw bands a half turn, then take 1 hour to bring water to simmering (170°F.). Retain for 30 minutes for large jars or bottles, or 20 minutes for smaller ones.
8 Lift out carefully, stand on a wooden surface and tighten screw bands.
9 Tie adhesive tape round the corks or caps of cordial bottles.

To use fruit syrups

Fruit syrups can be used diluted with water or soda water in cold drinks with milk for milk shakes, or poured over ice cream or cold moulds.

Blackberry syrup

you will need:

To each 1 lb. fruit:	*To each 1 pint juice:*
¼ pint water	8–12 oz. sugar

Method as for Fruit syrups (see above).

Blackcurrant syrup

(illustrated on the cover)

you will need:

To 1 lb. blackcurrants:	To 1 pint juice:
¼ pint water	8–12 oz. sugar

Proceed as for Fruit syrups (see page 52).

Cherry syrup

you will need:

very ripe juicy black
  cherries

To 1 lb. fruit:	To 1 pint juice:
¼ pint water	8–12 oz. sugar

Method as for Fruit syrups (see page 52).

Damson syrup

you will need:

To 1 lb. fruit:	To 1 pint juice:
⅜ pint water	12 oz. sugar

Method as for Fruit syrups (see page 52).

Elderberry syrup

you will need:

To 1 lb. elderberries:	To 1 pint juice:
¼ pint water	8 oz. sugar

Follow direction for Fruit syrups (see page 52).

Lemonade syrup

you will need:

8 lemons	To 1 pint juice:
½ pint water	8–12 oz. sugar

1 Thinly peel the lemons.
2 Put peel into a pan with the water.
3 Simmer for 5 minutes.
4 Strain and add to the lemon juice.
5 Measure and add the sugar.
6 Proceed as step 3 in Fruit syrups (see page 52).

Lemon ginger syrup

you will need:

1 lemon	To 1 pint liquid:
4 oz. bruised whole	1 lb. sugar
ginger	juice 1 small lemon
2 pints water	

1 Thinly peel the rind of the lemon.
2 Put ginger into a saucepan with the water and lemon rind.
3 Bring to the boil and boil slowly for about 45 minutes.
4 Strain, measure, and add sugar and lemon juice.
5 Put the liquid, sugar and lemon into a saucepan and boil for 10 minutes, skimming well.
6 When cold, put into bottles and seal.
7 When required put a tablespoon of the syrup into a tumbler and fill up with boiling water.
8 Put a thin slice lemon on top and serve at once.

Loganberry syrup

you will need:

To 1lb. loganberries:	To 1 pint juice:
2 tablespoons water	8–12 oz. sugar

Method as for Fruit syrups (see page 52).

Orangeade syrup

you will need:

12 oranges	To 1 pint juice:
½ pint water	8–12 oz. sugar

Follow directions for Lemonade syrup.

Raspberry syrup

you will need:

1 lb. raspberries	To 1 pint juice:
	8–12 oz. sugar

No water is needed for this recipe.

Method as for Fruit syrups (see page 52).

Redcurrant syrup

you will need:

To 1 lb. fruit:	To 1 pint juice:
¼ pint water	8–12 oz. sugar

Method as for Fruit syrups (see page 52).

Strawberry syrup

you will need:

1 lb. strawberries	*To 1 pint juice:*
	8–12 oz. sugar

No water is needed for this recipe.

Method as for Fruit syrups (see page 52).

Sugar syrup

you will need:

1 lb. sugar	¼ pint water

1 Dissolve sugar in water over a gentle heat.
2 Cool and bottle for use.

Note

This sugar syrup is better than plain sugar for sweetening drinks.

Fruit juices

These are made and prepared in exactly the same way as the fruit syrups, but are meant to be served undiluted, so use 2–4 oz. sugar to each pint of juice. They are most refreshing and make an ideal drink with ice.

Rose hip syrup

you will need:

1 lb. rose hips	*To 1 pint juice:*
3 pints boiling water	8–12 oz. sugar

1 Quickly grate or chop the hips and use immediately after grating.
2 Put into the boiling water.
3 Simmer for 5 minutes only.
4 Stand for 15 minutes.
5 Strain and measure.
6 Add the sugar and proceed from step 3 in Fruit syrups (see page 52).

The above method ensures that the maximum amount of vitamin C is preserved.

Rhubarb syrup

you will need:

To 1 lb. fruit:	*To 1 pint juice:*
¼ pint water	12 oz. sugar:

Method as for Fruit syrups (see page 52).

Cold Milk Drinks

Cold milk drinks can be very varied. Since most members of the family love chocolate flavours, there are a number of variations of chocolate.

Milk shakes, which are very easy to produce, are also given.

Iced chocolate

you will need for 1 glass:

2 teaspoons drinking chocolate	⅓ pint milk
1 teaspoon boiling water	

1 Blend chocolate with the boiling water and mix to a smooth consistency.
2 Pour in the milk and whisk well.
3 Pour into glass and serve ice cold.

Iced chocolate cream

you will need for 1 glass:

2 teaspoons drinking chocolate	⅓ pint milk
1 teaspoon boiling water	fresh whipped cream

1 Mix the chocolate to a smooth consistency with the boiling water.
2 Pour in the milk and whisk thoroughly.
3 Pour into glass and top with cream.

Iced chocolate orange

you will need for 1 glass:

2 teaspoons drinking chocolate	⅓ pint iced milk
1 teaspoon boiling water	1 tablespoon canned orange juice

1 Put the chocolate into a measure and add the boiling water.
2 Stir well and mix in the iced milk.
3 Add the orange juice and whisk well.
4 Serve in a glass.

Iced chocolate pop

you will need for 1 glass:

2 teaspoons drinking chocolate
1 teaspoon boiling water
¼ pint iced milk
ginger beer

1 Put the chocolate into a measure.
2 Add the boiling water and stir well.
3 Stir in the iced milk.
4 Top up to ⅓ pint with ginger beer.
5 Whisk and serve.

Iced chocolate with treacle

you will need for 1 glass:

2 teaspoons drinking chocolate
1 teaspoon boiling water
⅓ pint iced milk
1 teaspoon black treacle
2 ice cubes

1 Put the chocolate into a measure.
2 Add the boiling water and stir well.
3 Stir in a little of the milk, then the treacle.
4 Whisk in the rest of the milk.
5 Pour into a glass and further chill the drink by adding the ice cubes.
6 Whisk them round for a few seconds, but take out before serving.

Iced mallow chocolate

you will need for 1 glass:

2 marshmallows
2 teaspoons boiling water
2 teaspoons drinking chocolate
⅓ pint iced milk

1 Crush 1 marshmallow in the boiling water.
2 When it is dissolved, stir in the chocolate.
3 Add the iced milk and whisk until frothy.
4 Pour into a tall glass and float the other marshmallow on top.

Chocolate Costa Brava

you will need for 1 glass:

2 teaspoons drinking chocolate
1 teaspoon boiling water
¼ pint iced milk
1 orange

1 Put the drinking chocolate into a measure.
2 Add the boiling water and mix well.
3 Pour in the iced milk, stirring all the time.
4 Serve in a glass.
5 Sprinkle the zest from the orange on top and place a slice of orange over the rim of the glass.

Note

It is essential the milk is ice cold or the orange slice may cause it to curdle.

Chocolate ginger cream

you will need for 1 glass:

¼ pint milk
2 teaspoons drinking chocolate
1 dessertspoon syrup from jar preserved ginger
1 tablespoon double cream
chopped preserved ginger

1 Heat milk and when hot pour into a cup.
2 Whisk in the chocolate and stir in the ginger syrup while still very hot.
3 Carefully pour on the cream and top with preserved ginger.

Chocolate maraschino

you will need for 1 glass:

2 teaspoons drinking chocolate
1 teaspoon boiling water
⅓ pint milk
2 teaspoons juice from maraschino cherries
1 maraschino cherry

1 Put the chocolate into a basin and blend with the boiling water.
2 Add the milk and maraschino juice, whisking well.
3 Pour into a glass and top with a maraschino cherry.

Chocolate marshmallow float

you will need for 1 glass:

2 teaspoons drinking chocolate
1 teaspoon boiling water
⅛ pint milk
1 marshmallow

1 Put the chocolate into a basin and mix with the boiling water to a smooth consistency.
2 Pour in the milk and whisk thoroughly.
3 Pour into glass and top with a marshmallow.

Cool chocolate lime

you will need for 1 glass;

2 teaspoons drinking chocolate
1 teaspoon boiling water
⅛ pint milk
1 tablespoon lime cordial

1 Put the chocolate into a measure.
2 Add the boiling water and stir well.
3 Add the milk and stir well.
4 Stir in the lime cordial.
5 Whisk and serve.

Coffee lime

you will need for 1 glass:

1 teaspoon instant coffee powder
1 teaspoon boiling water
⅓ pint milk
1 tablespoon lime cordial

Method as Cool chocolate lime above.

Creamy rum egg nog

you will need for 2 glasses:

1 egg
1 tablespoon castor or icing sugar
2 tablespoons thick cream
3 tablespoons rum
good ½ pint cold milk

1 Beat the egg with the sugar until fairly thick and creamy in colour.
2 Gradually fold in the cream, do this gently, so there is no fear of it becoming too thick and buttery.
3 Add the rum, and then the cold milk.
4 Serve at once.

With ice: this is rather rich, so it can be poured over a little crushed ice which not only cools the drink but lessens the richness.

Egg and milk

you will need for 1 glass:

1 egg
sugar to taste
⅛ pint milk
grated nutmeg

1 Whisk the egg lightly with the sugar.
2 Whisk in the cold milk and pour into a tumbler.
3 Top with graded nutmeg.

Egg nog

you will need for 1 glass:

1 egg
4 tablespoons syrup from canned fruit
¼ pint milk
pinch salt

1 Beat egg well and mix with the syrup from canned fruit.
2 Add milk and salt.
3 Mix well, chill and serve in a glass.

Golden milk drink

you will need for 4 glasses:

1 pint milk
1 pint ginger beer or ginger ale

1 Half fill the glasses with cold milk.
2 Top with ginger beer or ale.

Iced almond chocolate

you will need for 1 glass:

2 teaspoons drinking chocolate
1 teaspoon boiling water
3 drops almond essence
⅛ pint iced milk
1 scoop vanilla ice cream

1 Put the drinking chocolate into a measure.
2 Add the boiling water and mix well.
3 Add the almond essence and pour in the iced milk, whisking all the time.
4 Pour into a glass and top with the ice cream.

Iced alpine chocolate

you will need for 1 glass:

2 teaspoons drinking chocolate	1/3 pint iced milk thick cream
1 teaspoon boiling water	grated dark chocolate

1 Put the drinking chocolate into a measure.
2 Add the boiling water and mix well.
3 Pour in the iced milk, stirring all the time.
4 Serve in a glass or cup and gently pour over a thick layer of cream. To make the cream stay on the surface, pour it over the back of a spoon on to the drink.
5 Sprinkle with grated chocolate.

Lemon cooler

you will need for 1 glass:

1/4 pint milk	1 small ice cream brick
1 teaspoon finely grated lemon rind, or level tablespoon lemon marmalade	

1 Pour the milk into a basin.
2 Add the lemon rind or marmalade and ice cream cut into small pieces.
3 Whisk thoroughly until blended and frothy.
4 Pour into a tall glass and serve at once.

Lime cooler

you will need for 1 glass:

1/4 pint milk	1 small ice cream brick
1 teaspoon lime marmalade	

1 Pour the milk into a basin.
2 Add the marmalade and ice cream cut into small pieces.
3 Whisk thoroughly together until blended and frothy.
4 Pour into a tall glass and serve at once.

Milk soda

you will need for 2 glasses:

1/2 pint cold milk	little sugar (optional)
1/2 pint soda water	

1 Half fill tumblers with cold milk.
2 Top up with soda water.
3 Add a little sugar if desired.

Mocha marshmallow float

you will need for 1 glass:

1 teaspoon drinking chocolate	1 teaspoon boiling water
1/2 teaspoon instant coffee powder	1/3 pint milk 1 marshmallow

1 Put the chocolate and coffee powder into a basin.
2 Mix with the boiling water to a smooth consistency.
3 Pour in the milk and whisk thoroughly.
4 Pour into glass and top with the marshmallow.

Orange mocha whip

you will need for 1 glass:

2 teaspoons drinking chocolate	1/3 pint milk whipped cream
1 teaspoon coffee extract	orange slices
1 teaspoon boiling water	

1 Blend the chocolate and coffee with the boiling water.
2 Stir in the milk and whisk thoroughly.
3 Pour into glass and top with fresh cream and slices of orange.

Peppermint whisk

you will need for 2–3 glasses:

2–3 drops peppermint essence	1 pint milk
2 tablespoons ice cream	4 peppermint creams

1 Whip the peppermint essence in the ice cream.
2 Put into the bottom of 2–3 tall glasses.
3 Top with the cold milk and peppermint creams.

Rocky mountain chocolate

you will need for 1 glass:

2 teaspoons drinking chocolate	1 teaspoon maple syrup
1 teaspoon boiling water	1/3 pint iced milk popcorn

1 Put the drinking chocolate into a measure.
2 Add the boiling water and mix well.
3 Stir in the maple syrup and then whisk in the iced milk.
4 Serve in a tall glass and sprinkle popcorn on top of the drink.

Spanish cooler

you will need for 1 glass:

¼ pint milk
1 level tablespoon
  fine shred orange
  marmalade or jelly
1 small ice cream
  brick

To decorate:
grated orange rind or
  few strips marmalade
  peel

1 Pour the milk into a basin.
2 Add the marmalade and ice cream cut into small pieces.
3 Whisk thoroughly until blended and frothy.
4 Pour into tall glasses and decorate with a little grated orange rind or marmalade peel.
5 Serve at once.

Variation

With floating ice cream: whisk in only half the ice cream and float the remainder, cut into small squares, on top of the drink just before serving.

Cold milk shakes

These can be made in a variety of ways:

1 You can sometimes buy special milk shake syrups from the grocers and these are whisked with cold milk.
2 Another way to make milk shakes is to buy flavoured ice cream and whisk it with the cold milk.
3 Fresh fruit can be blended with cold milk and a little ice.
4 Coffee or chocolate powder can be whisked hard with milk and a little ice if available.
5 Use a liquidiser (see page 60).
6 You can use a proper malted milk mixer.

Choc'n raspberry shake

you will need for 1 glass:

2 teaspoons drinking
  chocolate
1 teaspoon boiling
  water

1 teaspoon raspberry
  milk shake syrup
¼ pint milk

1 Put the drinking chocolate into a measure.
2 Add the boiling water and mix well.
3 Add the raspberry syrup and whisk in the iced milk.
4 Serve in a glass.

Iced banana shake

you will need for 4 glasses:

2 ripe bananas
1 small ice cream
  brick

1 pint milk

1 Peel and thoroughly mash bananas.
2 Cut ice cream into small pieces and put all the ingredients into a large bowl.
3 Whisk until well blended and foamy.
4 Serve in tall glasses.

Iced raspberry shake

you will need for 4 glasses:

4 oz. raspberries
little sugar

1 small ice cream brick
1 pint milk

1 Mash raspberries, adding sugar to taste.
2 Cut ice cream into small pieces and put all the ingredients into a large bowl.
3 Whisk until well blended and foamy.
4 Serve in tall glasses.

Iced strawberry shake

you will need for 4 glasses:

4 oz. strawberries
little sugar

1 small ice cream brick
1 pint milk

Method as Iced raspberry shake above.

Malt and orange milk shake

you will need for 1 glass:

¼ pint milk
1–2 teaspoons malted
  milk powder
½ teaspoon grated
  orange rind

1 tablespoon orange
  juice

Whisk all ingredients together.

Malted coffee milk shake

you will need for 1 glass:

¼ pint milk
1–2 teaspoons malted
  milk powder

1 teaspoon instant
  coffee powder

Whisk all ingredients together.

Malted chocolate milk shake

you will need for 1 glass:

⅓ pint milk
1–2 teaspoons malted
  milk powder

2 teaspoons
  sweetened chocolate
  powder

Whisk all ingredients together.

Raspberry milk shake

you will need for 2–3 glasses:

¼ pint raspberry juice
juice ½ lemon
1 tablespoon sugar

½ pint water
¼ pint canned
  evaporated milk

1 Mix together the raspberry juice, lemon juice, sugar and water.
2 Stir until the sugar has dissolved.
3 Add milk, shake or whisk well.
4 Chill and serve.

Strawberry milk shake

Use strawberry juice from canned strawberries in place of raspberries.

Blackcurrant milk shake

Use blackcurrant juice from canned blackcurrants in place of raspberries.

Hot Milk Drinks

Hot milk shakes

Make as cold milk shakes (see page 58), omitting ice or ice cream. Care must be taken that the acid fruit syrups and milk are whisked very hard together to prevent any possibility of curdling.

Chocolate Parisien

you will need for 1 glass:

2 heaped teaspoons
  drinking chocolate
⅓ pint boiling milk

2–3 teaspoons *crème
  de cacao*

1 Put the drinking chocolate into a cup.
2 Add the boiling milk and *crème de cacao*.
3 Whisk and serve.

Hot chocomallow

you will need for 1 glass:

⅓ pint milk
2 teaspoons drinking
  chocolate

2 marshmallows

1 Heat milk and when hot pour into a cup.
2 Quickly whisk in the chocolate.
3 Serve with marshmallows floating on top.

Mocha whip

you will need for 2–3 glasses:

¼ pint very strong
  coffee
2 teaspoons cocoa
  powder

sugar to taste
¾ pint hot milk

1 Blend the coffee and cocoa powder in a jug or basin, adding sugar to taste.
2 Let milk come to the boil.
3 Pour over the chocolate and coffee and whisk very firmly.
4 If wished return to the pan and heat again until a slight froth appears.

Peppermint fluff

you will need for 1 glass:

1 or 2 peppermint
  creams or little
  peppermint essence

2 or 3 marshmallows
⅜ pint milk (hot but
  not boiling)

1 Dissolve peppermint and chopped marshmallows in the milk.
2 Serve in a tall glass.

Spicy chocolate

you will need for 1 glass:

¼ pint milk
2 teaspoons drinking
  chocolate
1 tablespoon thick
  cream
pinch powdered
  cinnamon
1 cinnamon stick

1 Heat milk and when hot pour into a cup.
2 Quickly whisk in the chocolate.
3 Pour on the cream and top with a sprinkling of powdered cinnamon.
4 Serve with a stick of cinnamon.

Treacle posset

you will need for 2 large tumblers:

1 pint milk
2 tablespoons treacle
juice 1 lemon

1 Put milk into a saucepan and bring almost to boiling point.
2 Add the treacle and lemon juice and boil slowly until the curd separates.
3 Strain and serve hot.
This is an excellent winter drink.

Port wine egg nog

you will need for 1 glass:

1 egg
little sugar
¾ wineglass port wine
1 tablespoon brandy
¼ pint hot milk

1 Whisk egg and sugar until frothy.
2 Whisk in port wine and brandy.
3 Pour into tumbler and top with hot milk.

Ratafia chocolate cream

you will need for 1 glass:

¼ pint hot milk
2 teaspoons drinking
  chocolate
ratafia essence
few ratafia biscuits

1 Pour hot milk into a cup and quickly whisk in the chocolate.
2 Add a little of the essence.
3 Serve with ratafia biscuits floating on top.

Drinks Made With a Liquidiser

Using a liquidiser goblet

A liquidiser goblet or blender, as it is sometimes called, is part of an electric mixer and one of the jobs it does so successfully is to produce a variety of cold drinks. You can put whole fruit into the liquidiser and get a smooth, liquid mixture. It also considerably aerates the mixture. Because it works so quickly and efficiently a drink can be perfectly blended in 1–2 minutes.

In some recipes ingredients are added when the liquidiser is running at half speed. This makes it easier to emulsify everything to avoid undue splashing. However, where you have a liquidiser with a removable centre part take this out and add extra ingredients through the comparatively small space.

If your lid is all in one piece at the top of the liquidiser lift this slightly off the goblet and add the extra ingredients through this opening.

Hot drinks in your liquidiser

Many of the hot drinks in this book can be blended in the liquidiser goblet. Although this is generally made of toughened glass so it can stand very hot temperatures, if your liquid is very hot it is advisable to pour warm water into the liquidiser first, then throw it away leaving the goblet warmed.

Using ice in a liquidiser goblet

You will notice that mention has been made of crushed ice in the liquidiser. This need not be crushed very firmly, but if very large lumps of ice are used they could in time bend the blades.

Alcoholic drinks made with a liquidiser

Brandy egg nog

you will need for 2 glasses:

½ pint milk
3 teaspoons sugar
1 egg

2–3 tablespoons brandy

1 Place milk in liquidiser goblet.
2 Switch on half-full and add sugar, egg and brandy.
3 Switch on to full for 1 minute.
4 Switch off and serve.

Egg punch

you will need for 4 glasses:

¾ pint white wine
2 eggs
2 tablespoons sugar

4 tablespoons rum
additional white wine

1 Place the wine and eggs into the liquidiser goblet.
2 Switch on half-full and add the sugar.
3 Switch quickly to full and mix until foaming.
4 Add the rum, mix well, and switch off.
5 Pour into a punch bowl and slowly add warm white wine.
6 Whisk and serve in special glasses.

Old boys' egg nog

you will need for 1 glass:

4 tablespoons champagne
4 tablespoons cream or milk
1 egg
1½ measures grenadine

1 slice pineapple
½ peach (fresh or canned)
2 tablespoons crushed ice

1 Place all the ingredients into the liquidiser goblet.
2 Switch on to full for 2 minutes.
3 Switch off and serve.

Rum egg nog

you will need for 2 glasses:

½ pint milk,
3 teaspoons sugar

1 egg
2–3 tablespoons rum

1 Place milk in liquidiser goblet.
2 Switch on half-full and add sugar, egg and rum.
3 Switch on to full for 1 minute.
4 Switch off and serve.

Singapore flip

you will need for 1 glass:

¼ pint milk
1 portion vanilla ice cream

4 tablespoons rum
1 slice pineapple

1 Place milk and vanilla ice into the liquidiser goblet.
2 Switch to half-full for a moment.
3 Add the rum and pineapple and switch on full for a moment.
4 Switch off and pour into a glass.

Wine egg nog

you will need for 1 glass:

¼ pint red or white wine
1 egg

little sugar
very little crushed ice

1 Put all the ingredients into the liquidiser goblet.
2 Switch quickly to full.
3 Leave until foaming.

Non-alcoholic drinks made with a liquidiser

Barley sugar flip

you will need for 1 glass:

½ pint milk
1 or 2 squares crushed barley sugar

1 tablespoon vanilla ice cream
dash maraschino

1 Place the milk into the liquidiser goblet.
2 Add barley sugar and ice cream.
3 Switch on full for 2 minutes.
4 Add a dash of maraschino to taste.

Butterfly egg nog

you will need for 1 glass:

⅜ pint milk	2 teaspoons sugar
1 egg	2 tablespoons crushed
1 teaspoon chocolate	ice
powder	
2 teaspoons honey or	
raisins	

1 Place the milk and egg into the liquidiser goblet.
2 Switch on half-full and add rest of the ingredients.
3 Switch on full for 2 minutes.
4 Switch off and serve.

Chocolate egg nog

you will need for 1 glass:

⅜ pint milk	2 teaspoons sugar
1 egg	2 tablespoons crushed
2 teaspoons chocolate	ice
powder	

1 Place the milk, egg and chocolate powder into the liquidiser goblet.
2 Switch on to full and add the sugar and ice.
3 Switch off after 2 minutes.

Chocolate flip

you will need for 1 glass:

½ pint milk	1 heaped tablespoon
2 teaspoons chocolate	vanilla ice cream
powder	

1 Place milk and chocolate powder into the liquidiser goblet.
2 Switch to half-full and add the vanilla ice cream.
3 Switch on full for 1 minute.
4 Switch off and pour into a glass.

Mocha flip

you will need for 1 glass:

4 tablespoons milk	¼ pint strong cold
1 tablespoon	coffee
chocolate ice cream	

1 Place all the ingredients in the liquidiser goblet.
2 Switch on full for 1 minute.
3 Switch off and pour into a glass.

Strawberry flip

you will need for 1 glass:

4 tablespoons milk	2 tablespoons
2 or 3 tablespoons	grenadine
fresh strawberries	or fruit syrup
1 heaped tablespoon	dash maraschino
strawberry or	
vanilla ice cream	

1 Place the milk into the liquidiser goblet.
2 Add the rest of the ingredients.
3 Switch on to full for 1 minute.
4 Switch off and pour into a glass.
5 Serve with a straw and spoon.

Vita blanche

you will need for 1 glass:

½ pint milk	pinch salt
2–3 oz. sliced celery	little sugar
2 tablespoons sliced	
apple	

1 Place the milk in the liquidiser goblet.
2 Add the rest of the ingredients.
3 Switch on to full for 1 minute.
4 Switch off and serve.

Vita rosa

you will need for 2 glasses:

½ orange	2 tablespoons diced
½ pint milk	tomato
4 tablespoons mineral	1 teaspoon sugar
water	

To garnish:

parsley	spring onions

1 Peel orange and remove pips.
2 Cut very finely.
3 Place the milk into the liquidiser goblet with the mineral water.
4 Add rest of the ingredients and switch on full for 1 minute.
5 Switch off and serve in a glass garnished with parsley and spring onions.

Ice cream sodas made with a liquidiser

Ice cream soda

you will need for 1 glass:

½ pint soda water   1 heaped tablespoon
vanilla ice cream

1 Place ingredients into the liquidiser goblet.
2 Switch on half-full and then quickly to full.
3 Allow to mix well.
4 Switch off and serve.

Variation

With fruit: add 4 tablespoons fruit syrup or 1 tablespoon fresh fruit, and mix in the normal way.

Chocolate ice cream soda

you will need for 1 glass:

4 tablespoons drinking   1 tablespoon vanilla
chocolate powder   ice cream
4 tablespoons milk

1 Place ingredients into liquidiser goblet.
2 Switch on full for 2 minutes.
3 Switch off and serve.

Italian ice cream soda

you will need for 1 glass:

¼ pint soda water   1 tablespoon lemon
4 tablespoons cream   syrup
1 finely chopped   1 tablespoon vanilla
orange   ice cream

1 Place ingredients into the liquidiser goblet.
2 Switch on full for 2 minutes.
3 Switch off and serve.

Palace ice cream soda

you will need for 1 glass:

¼ pint soda water   1 fresh or canned
4 tablespoons milk   peach
1 portion vanilla ice   dash maraschino
cream

1 Place the soda water, milk and ice cream into the liquidiser goblet.
2 Switch on full and add rest of ingredients.
3 Switch off after 2 minutes.

Milk shakes made with a liquidiser

Apple milk shake

you will need for 1 large or 2 small glasses:

⅜ pint milk   1 finely chopped sour
1 tablespoon   apple
condensed milk

1 Put milk and consensed milk into liquidiser goblet.
2 Switch on and add the apple.
3 Switch off after 2 minutes.

Apricot milk shake

you will need for 2 glasses:

½ pint milk   2 teaspoons sugar
6 finely chopped   1 tablespoon crushed
apricots   ice

1 Place milk in liquidiser goblet.
2 Switch on and add rest of the ingredients.
3 Switch off after 2 minutes.

Banana milk shake

you will need for 1 glass:

1 large banana   1 or 2 heaped
½ pint milk   teaspoons crushed
ice

1 Cut banana into 3 or 4 pieces.
2 Place milk into liquidiser goblet.
3 Switch on and add banana and ice.
4 Leave for 1 minute.
5 Switch off and serve in a tall glass.

Blackcurrant milk shake

you will need for 2 glasses:

½ pint milk   1 tablespoon crushed
few blackcurrants   ice
sugar to taste

1 Place milk in liquidiser goblet.
2 Switch on and add the rest of the ingredients.
3 Switch off after 2 minutes.

Orange milk shake

you will need for 1 large or 2 small glasses:

¾ pint milk
1 tablespoon
  condensed milk

1 orange, pulped
little sugar if wished

1 Put milk and condensed milk into liquidiser goblet.
2 Switch on and add orange pulp and sugar to taste if wished.
3 Switch off and after 2 minutes.

Chocolate milk shake

you will need for 2 glasses:

½ pint milk
1–2 teaspoons
  chocolate powder

sugar to taste
1 tablespoon crushed
  ice

1 Place milk in liquidiser goblet.
2 Switch on and add the rest of the ingredients.
3 Switch off after 2 minutes.

Coffee milk shake

Method as above, using 1–2 teaspoons instant coffee powder in place of chocolate.

Raspberry milk shake

you will need for 2 glasses:

½ pint milk
few fresh raspberries
sugar to taste

1 tablespoon crushed
  ice

1 Place milk in liquidiser goblet.
2 Switch on and add the rest of the ingredients.
3 Switch off after 2 minutes.

Strawberry milk shake

Method as above, using a few fresh strawberries instead of raspberries.

Tutti frutti milk shake

you will need for 1 glass:

¾ pint milk
1½ tablespoons sweet
  syrup

½ banana
½ chopped pear

1 Place milk and syrup into the liquidiser goblet.
2 Switch on and add banana and pear.
3 Switch off after 2 minutes.

Fruit juices made with a liquidiser

Apple juice

you will need for 1 glass:

¾ pint soda water
2 tablespoons crushed
  ice

3 teaspoons sugar
4–6 oz. chopped apple

1 Place the soda water in the liquidiser goblet.
2 Add rest of the ingredients.
3 Switch on full for 1 minute.
4 Switch off and serve.

Grapefruit juice

you will need for 1 glass:

¼ pint soda water
¼ pint grapefruit juice

4 teaspoons sugar

1 Place the soda water and grapefruit juice in the liquidiser goblet.
2 Switch on full and add the sugar.
3 Switch off after 2 minutes.

Lemon and parsley juice

you will need for 1 glass:

¾ pint soda water
½ measure lemon
  juice

1 sprig parsley
1 teaspoon sugar

1 Place the soda water, lemon juice and parsley into the liquidiser goblet.
2 Switch on full and add sugar.
3 Switch off and serve.

Strawberry juice

you will need for 1 glass:

¼ pint soda water
6–10 good ripe
  strawberries

3–4 teaspoons sugar

1 Place the soda water and strawberries in the liquidiser goblet, switching to half-full for a moment.
2 Switch on full and add the sugar.
3 Switch off and serve.

With other berries: this recipe can be made with all kinds of berries. If syrup is used it should be in the proportion of 1 measure syrup to 5 measures soda water. If desired, a stronger drink can be made by putting only 3 measures of soda water in the liquidiser goblet and adding more soda water to taste.

Park orangeade

you will need for 1 glass:

¼ pint orangeade
1 measure orange
  juice

2 finely chopped
  apricots

1 Place the orangeade and orange juice in the liquidiser goblet.
2 Switch on full and add the apricots.
3 Switch off after 2 minutes.

Cocktails and Aperitifs

While some people are very fond of a mixture of flavours in a cocktail, the modern tendency is simply to have sherry, Dubonnet or Cinzano. However, there are a selection of alcoholic and non-alcoholic cocktails which will suit most palates.

Rules for cocktails

The blending of flavours in a cocktail is entirely a matter of personal taste. Do not imagine that because you are mixing various alcohols cheaper quality goes undetected. It is almost more important when you mix drinks to use first-class ingredients.
Below are a few suggestions which you may like to follow:—

1 Simply put the ingredients together with the ice into a cocktail shaker.
2 Shake vigorously and strain to make certain your drink is clear and has no pieces of ice in it.

To crush ice

You can buy special ice hammers, but for most households the easiest way to do this is to put the lumps of ice on a clean tea towel. Fold the tea towel over the lumps and crush with a light hammer or rolling pin.
The tea towel stops the pieces of ice flying about.

Bloody Mary

you will need:

tomato juice
vodka

few drops
  Worcestershire
  sauce or lemon
  juice

1 Almost fill a cocktail glass with tomato juice.
2 Add vodka to taste and a little Worcestershire sauce or lemon juice.
3 Stir well before serving.

Brandy sour

you will need for 1 glass:

2 tablespoons brandy
1 dessertspoon sugar
  syrup (see page 54)

1 dessertspoon lemon
  juice
little crushed ice
soda water (optional)

To decorate:
sprig mint

1 maraschino cherry

1 Put ingredients into cocktail shaker or blend.
2 Pour into glasses.
3 Dilute with a very little soda water if wished.
4 Decorate with the mint and the maraschino cherry.

Whisky sour

As above using whisky instead of brandy.

Rum sour

As above, using rum instead of brandy. A little syrup from canned apricots is good in place of the sugar syrup.

Bronx

you will need:

equal parts dry gin
French vermouth (dry)

Italian vermouth (sweet)
squeeze orange juice
crushed ice

1 Put all the ingredients together with the ice into the cocktail shaker.
2 Shake vigorously and strain.

Champagne cocktail

you will need for 6–8 glasses:

4–6 lumps sugar
few drops angostura bitters

1 lemon
little ice
iced champagne

1 Put the lumps of sugar into the serving bowl and very thinly sprinkle each lump with a few drops angostura bitters.
2 Take the rind off the lemon.
3 Squeeze the juice of the lemon over the lumps of sugar before adding the rind—this extracts the oil.
4 Add the ice and then the champagne.

Note

If you want to make this straight into the glasses, follow the same procedure using 1 lump sugar per glass. A little brandy or orange brandy could be sprinkled over the lumps of sugar in place of, or in addition to, the angostura bitters.

Daiquiri

you will need:

2 parts Bacardi or rum
1 part lime or lemon juice or squash

little ice
dash angostura bitter or grenadine

1 Put all ingredients in a cocktail shaker or blend.

Dubonnet cocktail

you will need:

1 part gin
1 part Dubonnet

crushed ice
small pieces lemon

1 Put the gin, Dubonnet and ice into the cocktail shaker or blend.
2 Serve with small pieces of lemon.

Gin fizz

you will need for 2 glasses:

¼ pint gin
1 tablespoon lemon juice

1–2 teaspoons sugar
1 egg white
soda water

1 Blend all ingredients except soda water together.
2 Pour into glasses and add soda water to taste.

Gin fruit cocktail

you will need for 4 glasses:

6 oranges
1 lemon
1 grapefruit

cherries
4–6 tablespoons gin
ice

1 Strain the juice from all the fruit into a jug and chill for 30 minutes in the refrigerator.
2 Garnish with cherries and slices of orange after adding gin.
3 Serve in tall glasses with ice.

Gin and French

you will need:

2 parts gin
1 part French vermouth (dry)

lemon or olive

Mix together and top with twist of lemon peel or an olive.

Gin and Italian

Use the sweet Italian vermouth in place of the French dry vermouth above and serve with a maraschino cherry.

Gin and mixed vermouth

As gin and French, but use mixture of French and Italian vermouths and decorate with either olives, lemon or cherry.

Gin and orange bitters

you will need:

1 part orange bitters
2 parts gin

orange or lemon peel

Mix together and serve with a twist of orange or lemon peel.

Manhattan cocktail (dry)

you will need:

1 part whisky	dash curaçao
1 part French vermouth (dry)	olive or lemon peel to decorate
dash angostura bitters	

1 Either blend together or put with crushed ice into a cocktail shaker.
2 Decorate with an olive or lemon peel.

Manhattan cocktail (sweet)

As above, using sweet Italian vermouth in place of French vermouth.
Decorate with a maraschino cherry.

Manhattan mixed cocktail

As above, using a mixture of dry and sweet vermouths.

Mint julep

you will need for 1 glass:

1 large sprig mint	crushed ice
little sugar	whisky

1 Put the mint, sugar, ice and whisky into glasses and leave in the refrigerator for some little time to become very cold.
2 Top with more crushed ice if wished.

Pink gin

you will need:

few drops angostura bitters	gin
	water (optional)

1 Put a few drops angostura bitters into the glass.
2 Turn this round so the glass becomes faintly tinged with pink.
3 Throw away any surplus bitters and add gin.
4 Dilute with water as wished.

Tomato juice cocktail

you will need:

To each 2 pints of cored and cut up tomatoes:	1 tablespoon sugar (optional)
4 whole cloves	½ teaspoon celery salt
4 slices onion	2 tablespoons vinegar or lemon juice
2 teaspoons salt	

1 Simmer ingredients together until soft and rub through a fine sieve.
2 If the cocktail is to be stored, heat to boiling point.
3 Pour into bottles and sterilise.

Bottled tomato juice

you will need:

tomatoes	salt and pepper
sugar	

1 Wipe and stem ripe tomatoes.
2 Cut them in halves and put, cut side down, in a saucepan, standing it at the back of a warm stove until the juice begins to flow.
3 Press down frequently with a wooden spoon and boil for 30 minutes.
4 Strain through a fine colander—a soup strainer is ideal—pressing all the juice and most of the pulp through, leaving only skin and pips.
5 Put the juice back on the stove, add salt, sugar and pepper to taste.
6 Boil for 15 minutes.
7 Pour into hot sterilized jars or bottles and seal at once.
8 Stand in pan of boiling water for 15 minutes.
9 Do not season the juice too highly, as more can be added when served.
This makes a most refreshing drink.

Vermouth Cassis

you will need for 16 glasses:

1 large bottle dry French vermouth	crushed ice
3 liqueur glasses Cassis	1 siphon soda water

1 Pour vermouth and Cassis over the ice and add soda water immediately before serving.
2 Serve well chilled.

White lady

you will need:

2 parts gin
1 part lemon juice
1 part Cointreau
crushed ice (optional)

1 Mix together or put with a little crushed ice into cocktail shaker.

Vodka white lady

Recipe as above but use vodka in place of gin.

Cider in cocktails

Cider makes a very pleasant cocktail, blended with gin, etc. Some very good ciders are rather more potent than one might imagine so should not be offered to young people in the mistaken belief that it is a young person's drink.

Cider cocktail (1)

you will need for 5–6 glasses:

$\frac{1}{4}$ pint gin
1 pint sweet cider
1 slice lemon peel
ice

Put into a cocktail shaker with a little ice and mix or stir together.

Cider cocktail (2)

you will need for 4–6 glasses:

1 liqueur glass Cointreau
$\frac{1}{4}$ pint gin
1 pint medium sweet or dry cider
ice

Put into a cocktail shaker with a little ice and mix or stir together.

Cider and brandy cocktail

you will need for 4–6 glasses:

$\frac{1}{4}$ pint brandy
1 pint medium sweet cider
$\frac{1}{4}$ pint lime juice
dash bitters
squeeze lemon
ice

Put into a cocktail shaker with a little ice and mix or stir together.

Dusky belle cocktail

you will need for 4 glasses:

$\frac{1}{2}$ pint medium sweet cider
$\frac{1}{2}$ pint Guinness

Put into a cocktail shaker with a little ice and mix and stir together.

Liqueur special cocktail

you will need for 5–6 glasses:

$\frac{1}{4}$ pint brandy, gin, rum or whisky
1 pint medium sweet or dry cider
1 liqueur glass Grand Marnier, Cointreau, Drambuie or Van der Hum, according to taste

Put into a cocktail shaker with a little ice and mix or stir well.

Rum and cider cocktail

you will need for 4 glasses:

$\frac{1}{4}$ pint rum
1 pint cider

Put into a cocktail shaker with a little ice and mix or stir together.

Sherry and cider cocktail

you will need for 4 glasses:

$\frac{1}{4}$ pint gin
$\frac{1}{2}$ pint medium sweet cider
$\frac{1}{8}$ pint dry sherry
$\frac{1}{4}$ pint orange squash
Cointreau to taste

Put into a cocktail shaker with a little ice and mix or stir together.

Spiced cider

you will need for 4 glasses:

6 cloves
3 inches cinnamon stick
$1\frac{1}{2}$ pints sweet cider*
$\frac{1}{2}$ teaspoon grated lemon rind
$\frac{1}{2}$ teaspoon grated orange rind

To garnish:
orange slices
cucumber slices

* By using a non-alcoholic cider, this can be used as a non-alcoholic drink

1 Mix the spices and half the cider.
2 Heat gently, until boiling point is reached.
3 Let steep for 30 minutes.
4 Add the rest of the cider and peel.
5 Chill and serve well iced.
6 Garnish with thin slices orange and cucumber.

Non-alcoholic cocktails

Mixed fruit cocktail

you will need for 3–4 glasses:

6 oranges	cherries
1 lemon	ice
1 grapefruit	

1 Strain the juice of all the fruit into a jug and chill for 30 minutes in the refrigerator.
2 Garnish with cherries and slices of orange.
3 Serve in tall glasses with ice.

Strawberry cocktail

you will need for 1 glass:

2 strawberries	1 teaspoon orange
little sugar	juice
1 tablespoon lemon	iced water or soda
juice	water

1 Slice the strawberries into the bottom of a glass.
2 Add the sugar, fruit juices and top up with iced water or soda water.

Pineapple cocktail

Recipes as above but use 1 tablespoon chopped pineapple instead of strawberries and little sugar if using fresh fruit.

Cold Cups and Punches

You will find that the drinks in this chapter serve two very useful purposes:

(a) They provide a delicious looking drink which is slightly unusual.

(b) They make your wines go further.

There are, however, certain basic points to remember.

1 You cannot mix together a whole selection of flavours however pleasant each one may be individually and expect to have a delicious drink. The flavours must be chosen with care. If you add a liqueur to a wine the liqueur must complement not form a contrast in flavour.
It has been pointed out that your wine will go further in a cup, but too much sugar syrup produces a rather sickly unappetising drink.

2 You need not use a very expensive wine, but if you are making it for a large number of people choose a medium wine as you do not know if they will all enjoy a very sweet drink or rather dry wine. The Rhine and Moselle wines are an ideal choice, so ask your wine merchant to tell you a little about these. A French Graves or Sauternes is also the basis of a good white wine cup. Here again when choosing a Sauternes do not have it too sweet.

3 Although in the recipes the mixing appears to be done quite quickly, you get a better blending of flavours if the ingredients can stand for a while. Soda water and ice are added just before serving.

4 The container in which you put your cup is important—have this very cold and if possible choose a colour that enhances the colour of the liquid.

5 Your attractive garnishes make a great deal of difference. Do not cut the peel off oranges, apples or cucumber. Try to find rather special lemon flavoured mint or use borage, etc.
In the following recipes the usual fruit are used, but there is no reason why other soft fruits should not be added to a cup. If they are just meant as a garnish they can go in at the end. If, however, they are an essential part of the cup, cut them into tiny pieces and place them in the container first so that the liquid, when poured over the top, draws out the fruit juices.

Apricot wine cup

you will need for 20 glasses:

1 lb. apricots	1 bottle vin rosé
2 oz. sugar	little lemon juice
¼ pint apricot brandy	ice or soda water
1 bottle dry white	(optional)
wine	

To decorate:
mint sprigs   slices cucumber

1 If the apricots are not very ripe, cut into neat slices and poach in a syrup made of ½ pint water, 3 oz. sugar and the juice of 1 lemon.
2 Pour into the bottom of a bowl and add the sugar and apricot brandy and leave for 1 hour.
3 Add the rest of the ingredients and serve as cold as possible, decorating with mint sprigs and cucumber slices.

This is almost more delicious if served without ice or soda water, and very well chilled. It is, however, very potent and you may like to dilute by adding crushed ice and a little soda water just before serving.

Brandy tea cup

you will need for 8 glasses:

1 pint moderately	⅛ pint lemon juice
strong tea	crushed ice
½ pint brandy	lemon slices
3 oz. sugar	

1 Very carefully strain the tea.
2 Put tea, brandy and sugar into a pan.
3 Bring to the boil and add lemon juice.
4 Allow to cool and add crushed ice.
5 Decorate with lemon slices and serve in bowl.

Brandy and rosé cup

you will need for 12–14 glasses:

1 bottle rosé wine	*To decorate:*
½ bottle red wine	selection of fruit—
¼ bottle brandy	sliced lemon,
To serve:	cherries, orange
ice cubes	slices etc.

1 Chill the bottles of wine and brandy well before making the cup.
2 Crush the ice cubes in a bowl, then add the chilled wine and brandy.
3 Top with the fruit.

Cider and brandy cup

As the brandy and rosé cup, but use dry cider instead of the vin rosé. As this does not give such a pleasant colour to the cup, add plenty of bright coloured fruit.

Champagne cup

you will need for 18 glasses:

rind and juice 2–3	3 oz. sugar
small oranges	½ pint water
rind and juice 2	3 pints champagne
lemons	ice cubes

1 Boil the orange and lemon rinds with sugar and water for 5 minutes.
2 Strain into a large bowl.
3 Add the fruit juices, champagne and ice cubes.

Champagne and cider cup

you will need for 8–10 glasses:

1 lb. strawberries,	2 liqueur glasses
sliced peaches or	brandy
other fresh fruit	ice
2 pints medium	sugar
sweet cider	1 pint champagne or
	other sparkling wine

1 Steep the strawberries or other fruit in the cider and brandy for an hour or longer before needed.
2 Just before serving add ice and sugar to taste.
3 Finally add the champagne or other wine.

Cherry wine cup

you will need for 20 glasses:

1 lb. cherries	*To decorate:*
2 oz. sugar	mint sprigs
¼ pint cherry brandy	slices cucumber
2 bottles vin rosé	
little lemon juice	

Method as for Apricot wine cup.

Cider wine cup

you will need for 15–20 glasses:

1 medium sized can pineapple chunks	1 pint red wine
3 oz. sugar	*To garnish:*
1 pint water	pineapple chunks
2 pints cider	2 sliced oranges
liqueur glass kirsch	little crushed ice

1 Strain the juice from the pineapple chunks.
2 Boil the sugar and water and add to the pine-apple juice.
3 Add the other ingredients.
4 Pour into a large bowl.
5 Garnish with pineapple, slices of orange and crushed ice.

Claret cup (1)

you will need for 8–20 glasses:

3 oz. sugar	2 pints claret
¼ pint water	ice cubes
rind and juice 2 lemons	soda water
rind and juice 2 oranges	

To garnish:

sliced cucumber	sliced apple or sliced
sprigs borage or mint	orange

1 Boil the sugar and water with the fruit rinds.
2 Strain over the fresh fruit juices, then add the claret.
3 Put ice cubes into a bowl and pour the mixture over.
4 Just before serving add soda water.
5 Garnish with the sliced cucumber, sprigs of borage or mint and the sliced apple or orange.

Claret cup (2)

you will need for 18 glasses:

rind and juice 2–3 small oranges	½ pint water
rind and juice 2 lemons	3 pints claret
3 oz. sugar	ice cubes
	1–1½ pints soda water

To decorate:
mint or borage

1 Boil the orange and lemon rinds with sugar and water for 5 minutes.
2 Strain into large bowl.
3 Add the fruit juices, claret and ice cubes.
4 Just before serving add the soda water and decorate with mint or borage.

Lemon rum cup

you will need for 14 glasses:

juice and rind 4 lemons	1 pint weak tea (preferably China)
½ pint water	1 pint soda water
4 oz. sugar	crushed ice (optional)
1 pint rum	

To decorate:

sliced lemons	sliced cucumber
borage	

1 Put the thinly pared rind from the lemons into a saucepan.
2 Add the water and simmer gently for about 8 minutes then strain.
3 Dissolve the sugar in the hot lemon liquid, then add lemon juice and rum and the well strained tea.
4 Allow to cool, add the soda water just before pouring into large bowl.
5 If using crushed ice omit a little soda water.
6 Decorate with the sliced lemons, borage, sliced cucumber.

This is a strong and expensive mixture, if wished only ½ pint rum can be used and a little more lemon juice and nearly 1½ pints tea.

Peach wine cup

you will need for 20 glasses:

1 lb. peaches	2 bottles dry white wine
2 oz. sugar	little lemon juice
¼ pint peach brandy	

To decorate:

mint sprigs	slices cucumber

Method as for Apricot wine cup (see page 70).

Pineapple wine cup

you will need for 20 glasses:

1 small pineapple	2 bottles dry white wine
2 oz. sugar	little lemon juice
¼ pint kirsch	

To decorate:

mint sprigs	slices cucumber

Method as for Apricot wine cup (see page 70).

Raspberry wine cup

you will need for 20 glasses:

1 lb. raspberries
2 oz. sugar
¼ pint raspberry or
  cherry brandy

2 bottles vin rosé
little lemon juice

To decorate:
mint sprigs   slices cucumber

Method as for Strawberry wine cup, right.

Rosé cup

you will need for 18 glasses:

rind and juice 2–3
  small oranges
rind and juice 2
  lemons
3 oz. sugar

½ pint water
3 pints vin rosé
2 wine glasses cherry
  brandy
ice cubes

1 Boil the orange and lemon rinds with sugar and water for 5 minutes.
2 Strain into a large bowl.
3 Add the fruit juices, vin rosé, cherry brandy and ice cubes.

Strawberry cider cup

you will need for about 8–10 glasses:

2 lb. strawberries—
  choose tiny ones
2 lemons
4 oz. sugar

¼ pint water
2 pints sweet cider
ice cubes

1 Put about half the strawberries into a saucepan with the thinly pared rind of the lemons.
2 Add the sugar and water, cover the pan and simmer for about 5–10 minutes, then gently press the strawberries to extract the juice.
3 Strain most carefully, then allow to cool.
4 Put the rest of the strawberries into a bowl with the lemon juice, strain the strawberry liquid over and add the cider and ice cubes.
5 This is a very refreshing drink, serve it with a spoon so the fruit is not wasted.

Note

This can be varied by using a dry cider, a non-alcoholic cider or white wine and orange juice and rind instead of lemon.

Strawberry wine cup

you will need for 20 glasses:

1 lb. strawberries
2 oz. sugar
¼ pint brandy

1 bottle dry white wine
1 bottle vin rosé
little lemon juice

To decorate:
mint sprigs   slices cucumber

1 Cut up approximately 12 oz. of the strawberries into neat slices or quarters.
2 Put at the bottom of a bowl with the sugar and brandy.
3 Leave for 1 hour.
4 Add the rest of the ingredients and serve as cold as possible, decorating with the remaining strawberries, mint sprigs and cucumber.

Note

Do not add crushed ice as this is a fairly potent wine cup.

Teenage cider cup

you will need for 18 glasses:

rind and juice 2–3
  small oranges
rind and juice 2
  lemons
3 oz. sugar
½ pint water

3 pints dry cider*
ice cubes
sliced oranges, apples,
  cucumber and mint
  (when obtainable)
1–1½ pints soda water

* If wishing to make this drink non-alcoholic make sure you are using non-alcoholic cider

1 Boil the orange and lemon rinds with sugar and water for 5 minutes.
2 Strain into a large bowl.
3 Add the fruit juices, cider and ice cubes.
4 Put sliced fruit, etc. on top if possible.
5 Just before serving add the soda water.

Sauternes wine cup

Recipe as above, but use sweet sauternes in place of cider.

Burgundy wine cup

Recipe as above, but use burgundy in place of cider.

Golden wine cup

you will need for about 12 glasses:

1 can orange juice (about 1 pint)	1 bottle white wine (or dry cider)
1 can pineapple juice (about 1 pint)	ice cubes
1 small can apricot halves or equivalent in cooked apricots	*To decorate:* apricot halves
1 lemon	sliced orange
	borage flowers

1 Chill the cans of fruit juice very well.
2 Strain the juice from the apricots and add this to the lemon juice in the bowl.
3 Blend with the chilled fruit juices, wine or cider and add the crushed ice.
4 Decorate with the sliced apricot halves, orange slices, then to make a complete contrast add the borage flowers.

Golden wine cup de luxe

Ingredients as above, but use double the amount of orange juice and omit the pineapple juice, use mandarin oranges instead of apricots.

Continue as stages 1–2 then add about 2 wineglasses of Orange Curaçao and decorate with sliced oranges and the mandarin oranges.

White wine cup

you will need for 13 glasses:

rind and juice 2–3 small oranges	3 pints rather dry white wine
rind and juice 2 lemons	2 wine glasses brandy or curaçao
3 oz. sugar	ice cubes
¼ pint water	

1 Boil the orange and lemon rinds with sugar and water for 5 minutes.
2 Strain into a large bowl.
3 Add the fruit juices, wine, brandy and ice cubes.

Apricot cup

you will need for 12–14 glasses:

1 medium can apricots	1 bottle vin rosé
2 oranges	*To decorate:*
2 lemons	1–2 oz. split almonds
1 bottle white wine	mint leaves

1 Chill all the ingredients, except the whole fruit, well.
2 Pare the rinds from the oranges and lemons and heat for about 5 minutes in the apricot syrup, strain.
3 Slice the apricots and put in the bowl with the rest of the ingredients and decorate.
4 If you wish to use ice cubes be rather sparing with these, as this has not a strong flavour, and too much ice can make it too weak.

Christmas champagne cup

you will need for 12–14 glasses:

rind and juice 1 lemon	¼ pint water
	ice
rind and juice 2 oranges	2 bottles non-vintage sweet champagne
3 oz. sugar	2 wineglasses brandy

To decorate:
slices orange and lemon

1 Boil lemon and orange rinds, sugar and water for 5 minutes.
2 Cool and strain over ice.
3 Add champagne, brandy and fruit juice.
4 Stir and decorate with slices of orange and lemon.

Claret punch

you will need for 12–14 glasses:

juice and rind 1 lemon	ice
juice and rind 2 oranges	2 bottles rather sweet claret
3 oz. sugar	2 wineglasses cherry brandy
¼ pint water	

To decorate:
slices orange and lemon

1 Boil lemon and orange rinds, sugar and water for 5 minutes.
2 Cool and strain over ice.
3 Add claret, cherry brandy and fruit juices.
4 Stir and decorate with slices of orange and lemon.

White wine punch

you will need for 12–14 glasses:

rind and juice 1
  lemon
rind and juice 2
  oranges
3 oz. sugar

¼ pint water
ice
2 bottles white wine
2 wineglasses apricot
  brandy

To decorate:
slices orange and
  lemon

1 Boil lemon and orange rinds, sugar and water.
2 Cool and strain over ice.
3 Add white wine, apricot brandy and fruit juices.
4 Stir and decorate with slices of orange and lemon.

Winter cream punch

you will need for 8–10 glasses:

2 jars or cans cream
2 teaspoons sugar
½ pint Madeira or
  similar wine

soda water
little brandy
  (optional)

1 Put the cream into a large jug and stir in the sugar.
2 Gradually blend in the Madeira or other wine.
3 Half fill glasses with the mixture and top with soda water.
4 A little brandy added to the mixture before adding the soda water gives extra luxury.

Barrier reef

you will need for 18 glasses:

2 bottles dry white
  wine
3 measures
  Commandaria
3 tablespoons quince
  liqueur

few de-seeded grapes
½ pint lemonade
crushed ice
sugar to taste

1 Mix together wine, Commandaria, quince liqueur, grapes and lemonade with the crushed ice.
2 When fairly well chilled, add sugar to taste.
3 Serve when very cold.

Cherie

you will need for 18 glasses:

1 bottle vin rosé
crushed ice
little fresh or canned
  stoned cherries
1 bottle sauternes

2 tablespoons cherry
  brandy
sugar to taste
¼ pint soda water

1 Pour vin rosé over ice, adding fruit.
2 Stir in sauternes, brandy and sugar to taste.
3 Immediately before serving add soda water.

Claret and sauternes frappé

you will need for 15–20 glasses:

strawberries to taste
1 bottle claret
1 bottle sauternes
2 liqueur glasses
  orange curaçao

2 tablespoons brandy
juice 3 lemons
sugar to taste
ice cubes
1 bottle soda water

1 Soak sliced fruit in wine.
2 Add liqueur, brandy, lemon juice, sugar and ice cubes.
3 Immediately before serving add soda water.
4 Serve well chilled.

Hock sparkler

you will need for 35–40 glasses:

1 lb. melon or other
  fresh fruit in season
sugar to taste
3 bottles hock
1 bottle sparkling
  hock

1 liqueur glass brandy
3 liqueur glasses
  orange curaçao
crushed ice
fruit to decorate

1 Cube melon or slice other fruit and place in bowl with sugar and still wine.
2 Leave for 1 hour.
3 Add remaining ingredients.
4 Serve slightly iced with piece of fruit and crushed ice in each glass.

Long bamboo

you will need for 20 glasses:

1 small grapefruit,
  diced
1 tablespoon diced or
  crushed pineapple
½ sliced lemon, diced

¼ pint brandy
juice 1½ lemons
4 oz. castor sugar
2 bottles chablis
cracked ice
2 pints fizzy lemonade*

To garnish:
cherries

mint

* The proportion of lemonade can be increased or omitted altogether if desired.

1 Soak all fruit in brandy.
2 Add lemon juice and sugar and stir well.
3 Add chablis and pour over cracked ice in punch bowl.
4 Half fill long glasses.
5 Top up with lemonade.
6 Garnish with cherries and mint.

Lunar julep

you will need for 30 glasses:

3 bottles white burgundy
3 tablespoons *crème de menthe*
¼ bottle pernod
crushed ice
sugar to taste
finely sliced thin strips cucumber peel
soda water to taste

1 Mix wine, *crème de menthe* and pernod with crushed ice and sugar to taste.
2 Add cucumber peel and soda water immediately before serving.

Pride of Oporto

you will need for 12 glasses:

1 lemon
1 bottle tawny port
¼ pint orange curaçao
thin lemon slices
1 siphon soda water

1 Squeeze juice of lemon into bowl.
2 Add port and curaçao.
3 Decorate with the lemon slices.
4 Leave for 20 minutes.
5 Fill glasses two-thirds full of mixture, topping up each glass with chilled soda water.

Rum milk punch

you will need for 12 glasses:

½ pint rum
3 pints ice cold milk
2–3 tablespoons sugar (less if wished)
little crushed ice

To decorate:
sliced cucumber
mint or borage

1 Blend the rum with the milk, sugar.
2 Pour over a little crushed ice and decorate with sliced cucumber and borage or mint leaves.

Sangria

you will need for 18 glasses:

2 bottles red wine
1 bottle lemonade
crushed ice
1 liqueur glass brandy
little fresh fruit in season (apple, orange, or strawberries)

1 Pour red wine and lemonade over ice.
2 Add brandy and fruit.
3 Serve when cold.

Spice island

you will need for 15 glasses:

soft brown sugar to taste
4 tablespoons brandy
1 bottle red burgundy
crushed ice
1 pint ginger beer

1 Dissolve brown sugar in brandy.
2 Add red burgundy and crushed ice.
3 Allow to stand for at least 1 hour.
4 Just before serving add the ginger beer.

Summer holiday

you will need for 12 glasses:

1 bottle dry white burgundy
2 wineglasses port
little crushed ice
¼ pint soda water

1 Mix together burgundy and port.
2 Ice well and just prior to serving add the soda water.

Cups and punches for teenage parties

The following recipes are ideal for teenage parties when you do not wish to serve alcohol. These cups and punches look attractive and are much more interesting than just an ordinary soft drink.

These cups can be made into alcoholic drinks by using alcoholic cider.

Cider cup

(illustrated on the cover)

you will need for 6–8 glasses:

3 oz. sugar
¼ pint water
rind and juice 2
  lemons
rind and juice 2
  oranges

2 pints non-alcoholic
  cider
ice cubes
little soda water

To garnish:
cucumber slices
sprigs borage or mint

apple slices
orange slices

1 Boil sugar and water with fruit rinds.
2 Strain over the fresh fruit juices.
3 Add the cider.
4 Pour into a bowl over ice cubes.
5 Just before serving add soda water.
6 Decorate with the slices of cucumber, sprigs of borage or mint and the sliced apple and orange.

Fresh fruit cup

you will need for 8–10 glasses:

8 oz. diced fresh fruit
little sugar
¼ pint lemon squash
¼ pint grapefruit
  squash

½ pint orange squash
2½ pints water
few ice cubes

1 Put fruit in a large bowl with sprinkling of sugar.
2 Blend the squashes in a large jug with the water.
3 Pour over the fruit.
4 Add ice cubes just before serving.

Fruit cup

you will need for 8–10 glasses:

3 oz. sugar
¼ pint water
rind and juice 2
  lemons
rind and juice 2
  oranges

ice cubes
1 pint unfermented
  apple juice
1 pint ginger ale
soda water

To garnish:
cucumber, apple or
  orange slice

sprigs mint

1 Boil sugar and water together with fruit rinds.
2 Strain over fresh fruit juice.
3 Put ice cubes into bowl.
4 Pour the mixture over the cubes adding the apple juice and ginger ale.
5 Add the soda water just before serving.

6 Garnish with the cucumber, apple or orange slice and sprigs of mint.

Hawaiian cup

you will need for 5–6 glasses:

6 oz. diced pineapple
few glacé cherries
1 pint canned or
  bottled pineapple
  juice

1 pint lemonade
ice cubes

1 Put pineapple and cherries into a bowl.
2 Mix pineapple juice and lemonade together.
3 Add ice cubes.

This can be served hot topped with very little grated nutmeg.

Mint and ginger cup

you will need for 10 glasses:

3 tablespoons
  chopped mint leaves
rind and juice 2
  lemons
¼ pint water

3 oz. sugar
2 pints ginger beer or
  ginger ale
little crushed ice

To decorate:
lemon slices

sprigs mint

1 Put the chopped mint leaves into a basin.
2 Thinly pare the lemons and simmer peel for 5 minutes with the water.
3 Strain and add the sugar, lemon juice and pour over the mint.
4 Leave for 1–2 hours, then add the ginger beer or ale.
5 Pour into the bowl over crushed ice and decorate with the lemon slices and mint.

Orange and cider cup

you will need for 4–6 glasses:

3 oranges
sugar to taste
1 pint non-alcoholic
  cider

1 pint soda water

To garnish:
orange slices

1 Squeeze the juice from the oranges and add a little sugar to taste.
2 Add the cider and soda water.
3 Decorate with slices of orange.

Orange and pineapple cup

you will need for 9 glasses:

1 pint pineapple juice (canned or fresh)	1 orange
1 pint orange juice (canned or fresh)	¼ pint water
2 lemons	little sugar (optional)
	crushed ice
	soda water (optional)*

To decorate:
orange slices   mint or borage

* This is a fairly concentrated mixture and if wished can be diluted with soda water as well as the crushed ice.

1 Mix together the pineapple and orange juice.
2 Pare the lemon and orange rinds very thinly.
3 Simmer with the water for 5 minutes, then add the juice of the orange and lemon to the pineapple and orange mixture.
4 Taste and add a small amount of sugar if wished, but if using canned orange and pineapple juice this should be sufficiently sweetened.
5 Add a little crushed ice before serving and decorate.

Spiced cider cup

you will need for 6 glasses:

1 2-inch cinnamon stick	¼ pint lemon squash
3 or 4 cloves	¼ pint orange squash
pinch ground nutmeg	1 pint non-alcoholic cider
grated rind 1 orange	soda water (optional)

To decorate:
1 thinly sliced apple

1 Simmer cinnamon, cloves, nutmeg and orange rind in the mixed squash for 10 minutes.
2 Strain through fine muslin and add the cider.
3 Serve really cold with thinly sliced apple floating on the top.
4 Add soda water if wished.

Chilled fruit punch

you will need for 16 glasses:

1 pint boiling water	⅜ pint orange juice
3 rounded teaspoons tea	1 pint pineapple juice
4 tablespoons lemon juice	4 oz. sugar
	ice
	1½ pints ginger ale

To garnish:
lemon slices   maraschino cherries

1 Bring the water to a full rolling boil.
2 Immediately pour over tea.
3 Brew for 5 minutes.
4 Strain—set aside to cool at room temperature.
5 Combine with fruit juices and sugar and chill.
6 Just before serving pour over large pieces of ice or add ice cubes and ginger ale.
7 Garnish with lemon and cherries.

Fruit punch

you will need for 16 glasses:

6 whole cloves	⅛ pint lemon juice
½ pint tea	2 pints water
¾ pint boiling water	crushed ice
¼ pint orange juice	
¼ pint loganberry or raspberry juice	

To garnish:
mint leaves   orange slices

1 Mix together the cloves and tea.
2 Pour over the boiling water.
3 Leave for 20 minutes, then strain.
4 Add the orange, loganberry and lemon juice and water.
5 Serve with plenty of crushed ice and garnish with mint leaves and orange slices.

Orange ginger punch

you will need for 20 glasses:

3 oz. sugar	1 can orange juice (approx. 1 pint)
1 pint water	2 pints ginger beer
1 can pineapple juice (approx. 1 pint)	

To decorate:

mint	2 sliced oranges
2 sliced apples	cucumber slices

1 Boil sugar and water together until it becomes a syrup.
2 Add to pineapple and orange juice, together with ginger beer.
3 Pour into bowl.
4 Decorate with mint, sliced apples, oranges and cucumber.
5 Serve with ice.

Orange and strawberry punch

you will need for 10–12 glasses:

6 oranges
1 lemon
¼ pint water

4 oz. sugar
2 pints soda water

To decorate:
strawberries   orange slices

1 Squeeze the juice from the oranges and lemon.
2 Grate rind and boil in the water for 5 minutes.
3 Dissolve the sugar in the boiling orange and lemon liquid. Add juice.
4 Strain and chill thoroughly.
5 Add soda water and decorate with strawberries and orange slices.

Peach punch

you will need for 12–14 glasses:

¾ pint boiling water
3 cloves
¼ pint strong Indian or China tea
¼ pint lemon juice (fresh or canned)

¼ pint orange juice (fresh or canned)
½ pint peach juice
1½ pints iced water
sugar to taste

To garnish:
mint leaves   peach slices

1 Add the boiling water and cloves to the tea.
2 Allow to stand for 20 minutes and strain.
3 Add all the fruit juices and dilute with the iced water.
4 Add sugar to taste and serve garnished with mint leaves and peach slices.

Raspberry ginger punch

you will need for 18 glasses:

1½ lb. raspberries
2 tablespoons sugar
2 pints ginger beer

2 pints soda water
mint
ice cubes

1 Crush most of the fruit with the sugar.
2 Pour on the ginger beer.
3 Just before serving transfer to bowl.
4 Add soda water, few whole raspberries and mint.
5 Put cubes of ice into glasses before serving.

Strawberry ginger punch

Method and ingredients as for Raspberry ginger punch above, using strawberries instead of raspberries.

Spiced Virginia punch

you will need for 9 glasses:

½ pint water
4–6oz. sugar
1 3-inch cinnamon stick
3–4 cloves
1 pint orange juice (fresh or canned)

¼ pint lemon juice
¼ pint grapefruit juice
¼ pint pineapple juice
ice

1 Put the water into a saucepan and simmer with the sugar and spices for 10 minutes.
2 Strain off and chill as thoroughly as possible.
3 Mix in the chilled fruit juices and ice before serving if possible.

Hot Punches

Serving hot punches or cups

Today very few homes have a real punch bowl but a large ornamental mixing bowl or even the traditional cream coloured mixing bowl, ovenproof glass ware, etc., can suffice. If possible try to keep the drink hot by standing it on a hot-plate. Choose really solid glasses to take the drink.

A hot punch is ideal to welcome friends in cold weather. Remember you are blending rather potent ingredients, so do not serve too lavish an amount.

Apple honey punch

you will need for 3–4 glasses:

1 20–oz. bottle pure apple juice	pinch powdered cinnamon
3–4 level tablespoons honey	1 strip thinly sliced lemon peel
4 cloves	2 strips thinly sliced orange peel
1 3-inch cinnamon stick	

1 Place all ingredients in a saucepan.
2 Heat gently until the liquid begins to froth.
3 Leave to infuse for 10 minutes on a low heat. The punch must not be allowed to boil or even simmer.
4 Strain into a hot jug.
5 Pour into glasses and serve at once.

Bitter orange punch

you will need for 20 glasses:

3 large Seville or bitter oranges	½ pint brandy
1 pint water	⅛ pint curaçao
4 oz. sugar	½ pint weak tea (China is preferable)

To decorate:
little grated nutmeg

1 Pare the rind very thinly from the oranges, take care to use no pith at all.
2 Simmer with the water for 10 minutes, do not strain.
3 Add the sugar, brandy, curaçao, tea and orange juice and heat.
4 Pour into a hot punch bowl and decorate with the grated nutmeg.

Brandy punch

you will need for 12 glasses:

½ pint brandy	2 oz. sugar
1 pint ale	thinly pared rind 1 lemon
½ pint water	

To decorate:
grated nutmeg

1 Put all the ingredients into a pan.
2 Bring to the boil and taking care it does not continue to boil, keep hot until just ready to serve.
3 Pour into a hot punch bowl and top with grated nutmeg.

Brandy port punch

you will need for 12–16 glasses:

¾ pint water	¼ pint port wine
3 oz. sugar	2 pints light ale
rind 3 lemons	juice 2 lemons
¼ pint brandy	

To garnish:
little grated nutmeg

1 Put the water, sugar and lemon rind into a pan and simmer for 5 minutes.
2 Stir in the other ingredients and heat gently without boiling.
3 Pour into a hot punch bowl.
4 Sprinkle grated nutmeg over the top.

Kent brandy punch

you will need for 8–10 glasses:

2 lb. really ripe black cherries	2–3 oz. sugar
2 lemons	1 bottle red wine
½ pint water	1 miniature of brandy (2 if wished)

1 Stone the cherries; the easiest way to do this is to insert the bent end of a fine new hairpin into each cherry and pull out the stone sharply; do this over a saucepan so no juice is wasted.
2 Put the pared rind of the lemons and the water and sugar into the saucepan then simmer for about 10 minutes.
3 Remove the lemon rind, add the red wine and the cherries and heat gently, but do not let the cherries become 'cooked'.
4 Add the brandy and pour into a well warmed punch bowl.
5 Serve every guest with a spoon, for the piping hot cherries are delicious to eat.

Note

The above amount more than fills the number of glasses given because of the space taken by the fruit; if wished use just a few cherries and serve the rest for a dessert.

Kent cherry cup

Use the ingredients as for the punch, but I prefer vin rosé instead of red wine and cherry brandy instead of ordinary brandy. Heat the cherries as instructed, for this 'brings out' the flavour, then allow to cool, add the brandy and pour over crushed ice and serve.

Spanish apricot punch

Use about 1½ lb. fresh apricots instead of the cherries in the Kent cherry punch, and use a Spanish white wine instead of red wine. This is very good indeed, for it looks rather cool and pretty, but is very good hot.

Brandy and rum punch

you will need for 12 glasses:

½ pint brandy	½ pint ale
½ pint rum	2 oz. sugar
½ pint water	thinly pared rind 1 lemon

To decorate:
grated nutmeg

1 Put all the ingredients into a pan.
2 Bring to the boil and taking care it does not continue to boil, keep hot until just ready to serve.
3 Pour into a hot punch bowl and top with grated nutmeg.

Brandy tea punch

you will need for 8 glasses:

1 pint moderately strong tea	3 oz. sugar
½ pint brandy	⅛ pint lemon juice

To decorate:
lemon slices

1 Strain the tea very carefully.
2 Put with the brandy and sugar into a pan.
3 Bring to the boil and add lemon juice.
4 Heat, but do not boil again.
5 Pour into hot punch bowl and decorate with lemon slices.

Cardinal punch

you will need for 16 glasses:

1 large orange	*To decorate:*
6 cloves	grated nutmeg
2 bottles claret	

1 Put the cloves into the orange.
2 Bake in a hot oven until golden brown.
3 Cut orange into 6 portions with a clove in each.
4 Put into a pan with the claret and heat together.
5 Pour into a hot punch bowl.
6 Top with grated nutmeg.

Cider punch

you will need for 18 small cups:

few cloves	4 oz. sugar
1 large orange	3 pints cider*
rind and juice 2 lemons	1 teaspoon spice
½ pint water	½ teaspoon ginger
	grated nutmeg

* If wished, non-alcoholic cider may be used to give a less potent punch.

1 Put cloves into the orange and bake in oven for a while until it smells strongly.
2 Slice into hot bowl.
3 Boil lemon rind with water for 5 minutes.
4 Strain and add liquid to sugar, cider, spice, ginger and lemon juice.
5 Bring to the boil.
6 Pour into bowl and top with grated nutmeg.
7 Serve piping hot.

Cinnamon cider punch

you will need for 12–14 glasses:

3½ pints boiling water	2 pints medium sweet cider
2 teaspoons tea	8 oz. sugar
little grated lemon peel	¼ pint rum
1 teaspoon powdered cinnamon	

1 To the water add the tea, lemon peel and cinnamon.
2 Allow to draw for 5 minutes.
3 Strain into a bowl.
4 Gently heat the cider with the sugar and rum.
5 Add to the tea.
6 Serve piping hot.

Ginger punch

you will need for 5–6 glasses:

2 oz. diced crystallised ginger	¼ pint lemon squash
1 lemon	1 pint water
1½ pints ginger ale	2–3 oz. sugar

To decorate:
grated nutmeg

1 Put ginger and thinly sliced lemon into warm punch bowl.
2 Heat all other ingredients together.
3 Pour over the ginger and lemon.
4 Serve piping hot and decorate with grating of nutmeg.

Negus (1)

you will need for 12 glasses:

1 bottle port wine	grated nutmeg
½ pint water	½ teaspoon vanilla
2 oz. loaf sugar	essence or 1 vanilla
1 large lemon	pod

1 Put the port wine and water into a saucepan.
2 Rub the loaf sugar very firmly over the lemon to remove the yellow 'zest', add to the port wine and water.
3 Put in the lemon juice, nutmeg and vanilla.
4 Heat and pour into hot glasses or a hot bowl. Remove the vanilla pod before serving.

Negus (2)

you will need for 1 glass:

¼ pint port wine	sugar (optional)
¼ pint water	
2 tablespoons lemon juice	

1 Heat wine, water and juice.
2 A little sugar can be added if wished.
3 Serve hot.

Old fashioned Christmas punch

you will need for 12–18 glasses:

2 pints water	½ bottle rum
6–8 oz. sugar	½ bottle port wine
juice and rind 3 lemons	

To decorate:

nutmeg, grated	1 orange, sliced
1 apple, sliced	

1 Boil water, sugar and lemon rind together.
2 Strain.
3 Add rum, port wine, and lemon juice.
4 Pour into hot bowl.
5 Decorate with fruit and nutmeg.

Hot rum punch

Recipe as above, but use 1 bottle rum in place of port wine.

Orange and claret punch

you will need for 12 glasses:

12 cloves	little sugar to taste
2 oranges	grated nutmeg
2 bottles claret	

1 Put the cloves into the oranges and bake in a hot oven for about 15 minutes.
2 Put into a saucepan with the claret and a little sugar.
3 Bring to the boil, but do not continue boiling.
4 Pour into a hot punch bowl and top with grated nutmeg.

Orange and whisky punch

you will need for 7–8 glasses:

1 bottle whisky	⅛ pint orange juice
½ pint water	orange slices
2–3 oz. sugar	grated cinnamon

1 Put the whisky and water into a pan.
2 Heat and add sugar and orange juice.
3 Heat again without boiling.
4 Pour into a hot punch bowl and top with orange slices and grated cinnamon.

Port and orange punch

you will need for 16 glasses:

12 cloves	little sugar to taste
2 oranges	grated nutmeg
2 bottles port wine	

1 Put the cloves into the oranges and bake in a hot oven for about 15 minutes.
2 Put into a saucepan with the wine and a little sugar.
3 Bring to the boil, but do not continue boiling.
4 Pour into a hot punch bowl and top with grated nutmeg.

Rum punch

you will need for 14 glasses:

1 pint rum	$\frac{1}{8}$ pint lemon juice
1 pint ale	3 oz. sugar
$\frac{1}{4}$ pint water	grated nutmeg

1 Put all the ingredients into a pan.
2 Bring to the boil, and, taking care it does not continue to boil, keep hot until just ready to serve.
3 Pour into a hot punch bowl and top with grated nutmeg.

Coffee rum punch

you will need for about 8 glasses:

1$\frac{1}{2}$ pints moderately strong coffee	about $\frac{1}{4}$ pint thick cream
cinnamon stick	grated nutmeg or cinnamon
8 tablespoons rum	

1 Heat the coffee (strained from the coffee grounds) with the cinnamon for about 5 minutes; if it has become a little strong dilute with water to give the 1$\frac{1}{2}$ pints again.
2 Add the rum and heat gently, then serve in warmed glasses.
3 Top each glass with the cream—this looks better if whipped, but it does make it more difficult to drink.
4 Top with the grated nutmeg or cinnamon and serve at once. If wished put into a punch bowl and just serve topped with the grated spices and hand bowls of cream separately.

Creamed brandy punch

Follow the recipe above, but infuse the coffee with strips of lemon and not cinnamon.
Add brandy instead of rum.

Taronga twist

you will need for 14 glasses:

1 bottle sweet sherry (Australian sherry is perfect for this)	$\frac{1}{4}$ pint grapefruit juice
	1 sliced lemon
2 tablespoons brandy	1 small can pineapple, chopped small
4 oz. castor sugar	
4 tablespoons apricot brandy	

1 Heat together the sherry, brandy, sugar and apricot brandy.
2 Then add the grapefruit juice, lemon and chopped pineapple.
3 Serve hot.
4 To make this drink go further, $\frac{1}{4}$ hot water can be added to $\frac{3}{4}$ mixture.

Whisky punch

you will need for 7–8 glasses:

1 bottle whisky	2–3 oz. sugar
$\frac{1}{2}$ pint water	lemon slices
$\frac{1}{8}$ pint lemon juice	grated cinnamon

1 Put the whisky and water into a pan.
2 Heat and add lemon juice and sugar.
3 Heat again without boiling.
4 Pour into a hot punch bowl and top with slices lemon and grated cinnamon.

Wassail Bowls

Wassail is a hot drink that one serves at Christmas time. It was traditional to have it all ready, with mince pies, for the parties who came round singing carols. Any of the hot punches would be suitable for your Wassail bowl.

Mulled Drinks

Mulled ale was a drink which some years ago provided the 'spirit of Christmas'. The host would plunge a red hot poker into the bowl of spicy hot liquid to give a wonderful sound. In these days of modern heating, red hot pokers, of course, may not be easily obtainable, but you can still make a mulled drink as these recipes show.

Because it is a spicy drink, red wine or ale are the most suitable.

Mulled ale (1)

you will need for 8–9 glasses:

2 pints good ale
1 glass rum or brandy
1 tablespoon sugar
pinch ground cloves
pinch powdered ginger

1 Heat all ingredients together.
2 Serve in hot glasses or in a hot bowl.

Mulled ale (2)

you will need for 12 glasses:

1 large orange
6 cloves
3 pints old ale
¼ pint brandy or rum
good pinch powdered ginger
good pinch cinnamon
1 tablespoon sugar

1 Put the cloves into the orange and bake in a hot oven for about 15 minutes to give a stronger flavour to the peel.
2 Put into a large pan with all the other ingredients and bring to boiling point.
3 Pour into a hot silver punch bowl, and just before serving plunge a red hot clean poker into the drink.

Mulled burgundy

you will need for 8–10 glasses:

1 pint water
4 oz. granulated sugar
4 sticks cinnamon
4 cloves
2 lemons
1 bottle burgundy

1 Boil water with sugar, cinnamon and cloves for 5 minutes.
2 Add lemon thinly sliced and allow to stand for 10 minutes.

3 Add wine and heat slowly but do not allow to boil.
4 Put into a jug and serve very hot.

Note

A silver spoon in each glass will prevent it from cracking.

Mulled claret

you will need for 8 glasses:

1 bottle claret
3 tablespoons brandy
¼ pint water
2 oz. sugar
1 nutmeg
thinly pared rind 1 orange

1 Put the claret, brandy, water, sugar and nutmeg into a saucepan.
2 Heat gently until the sugar has dissolved, making sure the liquid is really hot and pour into hot glasses, removing the nutmeg.
3 Put a small piece of orange rind into each glass.

Mulled port

you will need:

1 bottle port
thinly pared rind 1 lemon
1 2-inch stick cinnamon
grating nutmeg
1 tablespoon sugar
¼ pint water

1 Put all the ingredients into a saucepan.
2 Bring just to boiling point, remove the cinnamon stick.
3 Pour into a hot bowl or hot glasses.

Mulled red wine

you will need for 10 glasses:

2 oz. sugar
¾ pint water
1 bottle burgundy
2 tablespoons honey
1–2 sliced lemons
grated nutmeg

1 Boil sugar and water.
2 Add burgundy and honey.
3 Heat without boiling again.
4 Pour over sliced lemon and top with grated nutmeg.

Toddies

A toddy is a very soothing winter drink, which is considered by many people to be one of the best ways of curing a cold or warming one after being out in cold weather.

Atholl Brose

you will need:

4 tablespoons fine
  oatmeal
little cold water

2–3 tablespoons honey
approximately 2 pints
  whisky

1 Blend the oatmeal with the water until a thick paste.
2 Very thoroughly mix with the honey and put into a large bottle.
3 Fill up with whisky.
4 Serve with hot or cold water or soda.

Ale posset

you will need for 1 glass:

¼ pint milk
¼ pint ale
2 teaspoons sugar

1 egg yolk
1 small piece crisp
  toast

1 Heat the milk in a saucepan together with the ale.
2 Stir in the sugar, and whisk in the egg yolk, but do not cook any further.
3 Pour over the toast into a tankard or rather solid glass.

Note

This is a good cold weather 'night cap'.

Apple toddy

you will need for 1 glass:

⅛ pint boiling water
2 tablespoons apple
  purée

little sugar
measure whisky

1 Pour the boiling water over the purée.
2 Strain to extract the juice.
3 Put into a saucepan with the sugar and add whisky.
4 Serve piping hot.

Note

This is very soothing for a cold.

Buttered rum

you will need for 4 glasses:

1 oz. butter
1 oz. brown sugar
little powdered
  cinnamon

⅜ pint rum
1 pint boiling water
1 lemon
grating nutmeg

1 Warm 4 glasses and divide the butter, sugar and cinnamon between them.
2 Add the rum and fill up with the boiling water.
3 Top with slices of lemon and a grating of nutmeg.

Rum Toddy

you will need for 1 glass:

1 teaspoon sugar
¼ pint hot water
squeeze lemon juice

1 measure rum
grated nutmeg

1 Dissolve sugar in hot water.
2 Add lemon juice and rum.
3 Heat and pour into a hot glass, adding little boiling water if required.
4 Top with grated nutmeg.

Whisky Toddy

you will need for 1 glass:

1 teaspoon sugar
¼ pint hot water
squeeze lemon juice
1 measure whisky

boiling water
  (optional)
grated nutmeg

1 Dissolve sugar in hot water.
2 Add lemon juice and whisky.
3 Heat and pour into a hot glass, adding little boiling water if required.
4 Top with grated nutmeg.

A Few Ideas for Party Food

As well as cocktail savouries, sandwiches are ideal party food. Tiny unusually shaped sandwiches will be very popular and these should, like all sandwiches, be kept covered with foil or damp cloths until the last minute, so that the bread does not dry. Try open sandwiches for a change—they look gay and attractive and can either be small enough for a cocktail party or large and sufficiently substantial for a main meal.

Canapés

These are ideal for cocktail parties. They are made from tiny pieces of toast, small biscuits, bread and butter or fried bread cut into small shapes and can be filled. Some suggestions are:
Small round biscuits (or rounds of fried bread), topped with butter, sliced hard-boiled egg, anchovy fillets and sliced stuffed olives. Heart-shaped pieces of fried bread topped with salami and sliced stuffed olives.
Diced Camembert cheese or diced Cheddar cheese topped with olives.
Baby sausage rolls.
Slices of salami rolled round gherkins.
Heart-shaped pieces of fried bread topped with same shaped pieces of cheese, cucumber rings and radish rings.
Rounds of fried bread or buttered biscuits, topped with a little mayonnaise and prawns.
Assorted shaped pieces of toast or fried bread topped with cream cheese, olives and walnuts.
Assorted shaped pieces of brown bread and butter or fried bread topped with smoked salmon.

Layer sandwiches

Layer sandwiches are made by putting several slices of bread and butter and two fillings together. Here are a few suggestions:
Mash two portions of Swiss Gruyère cheese with a little butter, 1 teaspoon French mustard and 2 chopped anchovies. Spread on alternate slices of white and brown (or black rye) bread.
Mix Swiss Gruyère cheese with chopped mint, chives and butter. Spread between brown and white bread.
Spread Swiss Gruyère cheese on buttered white bread, sprinkle with caraway seeds, spread with mayonnaise and thinly sliced tomato. Cover with buttered brown bread.

Hollow sandwiches

Take the tops off rolls, pull out the crumb, and rub this until very fine.
Mix with flaked tuna or other fish and diced Swiss Petit Gruyère cheese.
Use either oil from the tuna or mayonnaise to bind, and mix in chopped watercress or parsley.

Danish sandwiches

While small dainty open sandwiches can be served, the real Danish sandwiches are a meal in themselves. Cut reasonably thin bread, and vary this as much as possible—brown, white, wholemeal, and if possible look for rye bread, etc. in shops selling continental specialities. Make your open sandwiches look as colourful as possible. If prepared beforehand, cover with damp cloths or damp paper so that they keep fresh.

Suggested fillings for Danish sandwiches

Ham with asparagus tips—garnished with strips of pimento or tomato.
Sliced chicken topped with slivers of cucumber and creamed corn.
Potato salad topped with prawns or shrimps—garnished with a few French capers and slices of tomato.
Pickled herrings with onion rings. (Serve this on rye bread if possible).

Sausage rolls

cooking time   20–25 minutes

you will need:

$3\frac{1}{2}$ oz. whipped up
    cooking fat*
3 tablespoons cold
    water

8 oz. flour
$\frac{1}{2}$ level teaspoon salt
    sieved together
12 oz. sausage meat

* For specially rich pastry use 4 oz. whipped up
cooking fat and only 2 tablespoons water.

1 Place the whipped-up cooking fat in one piece,
water and 2 rounded tablespoons of the sieved
flour and salt into a basin.
2 Whisk together with a fork for about half a
minute until well mixed and fluffy.
3 Add remaining flour and stirring, form into a
firm dough. Very lightly knead with the finger-
tips on a lightly-floured board, moulding to a
smooth ball. A little kneading does not harm the
dough.
4 Roll out the dough, on a lightly-floured board.
into an oblong 12 inches × 6 inches. Trim
edges.
5 Divide into two 3-inch wide strips.
6 Roll three-quarters of the sausage meat into
two 12-inch sausages. Damp edges of pastry
strips.
7 Place the sausages in the centre of each strip;
fold over and press the long edges together.
8 Flake edges and mark tops diagonally with a
knife at $\frac{1}{4}$-inch intervals. Cut each diagonally
into six sausage rolls.
9 Repeat with the pastry trimmings and remaining sausage meat.
10 Place well apart on baking tray. Brush with
beaten egg and milk.
11 Bake near the top of a moderately hot oven
(400°F.—Gas Mark 6) for 20–25 minutes.

Trump crackers

cooking time   10 minutes

you will need:

white bread (several
    days old)
melted butter

finely grated Cheddar
    cheese
cayenne pepper

1 Using playing card cutters, cut thinly sliced
bread into shapes.
2 Dip them in melted butter and toss in finely
grated cheese to coat thoroughly.
3 Place on a baking sheet in a hot oven (425°F.
—Gas Mark 7) for about 10 minutes until a
rich golden brown.
4 Serve hot or cold.

Bacon titbits

Remove rind from streaky rashers, cut each
rasher in half, and spread with mustard or
chutney. Roll a piece of bacon round any of the
following: a cube of cheese or pineapple; a
cocktail sausage or a prawn; sweet gherkins or
stuffed olives; a piece of banana or a date. Place
on a cocktail stick, grill or bake until the bacon
is cooked. Serve hot or cold.

Ham bites

Spread thin slices of ham or lean bacon with
cream cheese or peanut butter, seasoned with
grated onion or horseradish sauce. Roll up
tightly, leave in the refrigerator or a cold place
for several hours. Cut into bite-sized pieces.

Index